✧   *Companions for the Journey*   ✧

Praying with
Catherine of Siena

✧ *Companions for the Journey* ✧

Praying with Catherine of Siena

by
Patricia Mary Vinje

Saint Mary's Press
Christian Brothers Publications
Winona, Minnesota

To Mom,

✧   *Phil, Marcia, Elizabeth, and Tom*   ✧

In Memory of Dad

The publishing team included Carl Koch, FSC, development editor; Rebecca L. Fairbank, manuscript editor; Gary J. Boisvert, typesetter; Elaine Kohner, illustrator; pre-press, printing, and binding by the graphics division of Saint Mary's Press.

The acknowledgments continue on page 109.

Printed in the United States of America

Printing: 7 6 5

Year: 1995

ISBN 0-88489-230-1

✧ Contents ✧

✧ Foreword ✧

Companions for the Journey

Just as food is required for human life, so are companions. Indeed, the word *companions* comes from two Latin words: *com*, meaning "with," and *panis*, meaning "bread." Companions nourish our heart, mind, soul, and body. They are also the people with whom we can celebrate the sharing of bread.

Perhaps the most touching stories in the Bible are about companionship: the Last Supper, the wedding feast at Cana, the sharing of the loaves and the fishes, and Jesus breaking bread with the disciples on the road to Emmaus. Each incident of companionship with Jesus revealed more about his mercy, love, wisdom, suffering, and hope. When Jesus went to pray in the Garden of Olives, he craved the companionship of the Apostles. They let him down. But God sent the Spirit to inflame the hearts of the Apostles, and they became faithful companions to Jesus and to each other.

Throughout history, other faithful companions have followed Jesus and the Apostles. These saints and mystics have also taken the journey from conversion, through suffering, to resurrection. Just as they were inspired by the holy people who went before them, so too may you take them as your companions as you walk on your spiritual journey.

The Companions for the Journey series is a response to the spiritual hunger of Christians. This series makes available the rich spiritual teachings of mystics and guides whose wisdom can help us on our pilgrimages. As you complete the last meditation in each volume, it is hoped that you will feel supported, challenged, and affirmed by a soul-companion on your spiritual journey.

The spiritual hunger that has emerged over the last twenty years is a great sign of renewal in Christian life. People fill retreat programs and workshops on topics in spirituality. The demand for spiritual directors exceeds the number available. Interest in the lives and writings of saints and mystics is increasing as people search for models of whole and holy Christian life.

Praying with the Saints

Praying with Catherine of Siena is more than just a book about Catherine's spirituality. This book seeks to engage you in praying in the way that Catherine did about issues and themes that were central to her experience. Each meditation can enlighten your understanding of her revelations and lead you to reflect on your own experience.

The goal of *Praying with Catherine of Siena* is that you will discover her profound spirituality and integrate her spirit and wisdom into your relationship with God, with your brothers and sisters, and with your own heart and mind.

Suggestions for Praying with Catherine

Meet Catherine, a courageous and fascinating companion for your pilgrimage, by reading the Introduction, which begins on page 15. It provides a brief biography of Catherine and an outline of the major themes of her spirituality.

Once you meet Catherine, you will be ready to pray with her and to encounter God, your sisters and brothers, and yourself in new and wonderful ways. To help your prayer, here are some suggestions that have been part of the tradition of Christian spirituality:

Create a sacred space. Jesus said, "But when you pray, go to your private room, shut yourself in, and so pray to your God who is in that secret place, and your God who sees all that is done in secret will reward you" (Matthew 6:6). Solitary prayer is best done in a place where you can have privacy and silence, both of which can be luxuries in the lives of busy people. If privacy and silence are not possible, create a quiet, safe place within yourself, perhaps while riding to and from work, while sitting in line at the dentist's office, or while waiting for someone. Do the best you can, knowing that a loving God is present everywhere. Whether the meditations in this book are used for solitary prayer or with a group, try to create a prayerful mood with candles, meditative music, a crucifix, or an image of Mary.

Open yourself to the power of prayer. Every human experience has a religious dimension. All of life is suffused with God's presence. So remind yourself that God is present as you begin your period of prayer. Do not worry about distractions. If something keeps intruding during your prayer, spend some time talking with God about it. Be flexible because God's Spirit blows where it will.

Prayer can open your mind and widen your vision. Be open to new ways of seeing God, people, and yourself. As you open yourself to the Spirit of God, different emotions are evoked, such as sadness from tender memories, or joy from a celebration recalled. Our emotions are messages from God that can tell us much about our spiritual quest. Also, prayer strengthens our will to act. Through prayer, God can touch our will and empower us to live according to what we know is true.

Finally, many of the meditations in this book will call you to employ your memories, your imagination, and the circumstances of your life as subjects for prayer. The great mystics and saints realized that they had to use all of their resources to know God better. Indeed, God speaks to us continually and touches us constantly. We must learn to listen and feel with all the means that God gave us.

Come to prayer with an open mind, heart, and will.

Preview each meditation before beginning. Spend a few moments previewing the readings and especially the reflection activities. Several reflection activities are given in each meditation because different styles of prayer appeal to different personalities or personal needs. **Note that each meditation has more reflection activities than can be done during one prayer period. Therefore, select only one or two reflection activities each time you use a meditation. Do not feel compelled to complete all of the reflection activities.**

Read meditatively. After you have placed yourself in God's presence, the meditations offer you a story about Catherine and a reading from her writings. Take your time reading. If a particular phrase touches you, stay with it. Relish its feelings, meanings, and concerns.

Use the reflections. Following the readings is a short reflection in commentary form meant to give perspective to the readings. Then you will be offered several ways of meditating on the readings and the theme of the prayer. You may be familiar with the different methods of meditating, but in case you are not, they are described briefly here:

✦ *Repeated short prayer or mantra:* One means of focusing your prayer is to use a *mantra*, or prayer word. The mantra may be a single word or a short phrase taken from the readings or from the Scriptures. For example, a mantra for a meditation on courage might be "I go before you" or "trust." Repeated slowly in harmony with your breathing, the mantra helps you center your heart and mind on one action or attribute of God.

✦ *Lectio divina:* This type of meditation is "divine studying," a concentrated reflection on the word of God or the wisdom of a spiritual writer. Most often in *lectio divina* you will be invited to read one of the passages several times and then concentrate on one or two sentences, pondering their meaning for you and their effect on you. *Lectio divina* commonly ends with formulation of a resolution.

✦ *Guided meditation:* In this type of meditation our imagination helps us consider alternative actions and likely consequences. Our imagination helps us experience new ways of seeing God, our neighbors, ourselves, and nature. When Jesus told his followers parables and stories, he engaged their imagination. In this book you will be asked to follow a guided meditation.

One way of doing a guided meditation is to read the scene or story several times until you know the outline and can recall it when you enter into reflection. Or prior to your prayer time, you may wish to record the meditation on a tape recorder. If so, remember to allow pauses for reflection between phrases and to speak with a slow, peaceful pace and tone. Then during prayer, when you have finished the readings and the reflection commentary, you can turn on your recording of the meditation and be led through it. If you find your own voice too distracting, ask a friend to make the tape for you.

✦ *Examen of consciousness:* The reflections often will ask you to examine how God has been speaking to you in your past and present experience—in other words, the reflections will ask you to examine your awareness of God's presence in your life.

✦ *Journal writing:* Writing is a process of discovery. If you write for any length of time, stating honestly what is on your mind and in your heart, you will unearth much about who you are, how you stand with your God, what deep longings reside in your soul, and more. In some instances you may be asked to write a dialog with Jesus or someone else. If you have never used writing as a means of meditation, try it. Reserve a special notebook for your journal writing. If desired, you can go back to your entries at a future time for an examen of consciousness.

✦ *Action:* Occasionally, a reflection may suggest singing a favorite hymn, going out for a walk, or undertaking some other physical activity. Actions can be meaningful forms of prayer.

Using the Meditations for Group Prayer

If you wish to use the meditations for community prayer, these suggestions may be of help:

✦ Read the theme to the group. Call the community into the presence of God, using the short opening prayer. Invite one or two participants to read one or both of the readings. If you use both readings, observe the pause between them.

✦ The reflection commentary may be used as a reading, or it can be deleted, depending on the needs and interests of the group.

✦ Select one of the reflection activities for your group. Allow sufficient time for your group to reflect, to do a centering prayer or mantra, to accomplish a studying prayer (*lectio divina*), or to finish an examen of consciousness. Depending on the group and the amount of available time, you may want to invite the participants to share their reflections, responses, or petitions with the group.

✦ Reading the passage from the Scriptures may serve as a summary of the meditation.

✦ If a formulated prayer or a psalm is given as a closing, it may be recited by the entire group. Or you may ask participants to offer their own prayers for the closing.

Now you are ready to begin praying with Catherine of Siena, a faithful and caring companion on this stage of your spiritual journey. For centuries, Catherine has been an inspiring guide for people seeking a closer relationship with God. It is hoped that you will find her to be a true soul-companion.

CARL KOCH, FSC
Editor

✧ Preface ✧

Catherine of Siena has held my interest since I first heard of her at the age of six. I can still remember the Dominican Sisters at Saint Bernard Grade School talking about this woman who vowed her life to God and yet lived in the house of her birth. Stories of Catherine's visions, fasting, and long periods of prayer fascinated me, and I am sure they shaped a lot of my ideas about God, saints, and prayer.

This book of meditations on Catherine gathers together the insights and reflections about her that have been developing inside me since my youth. I am grateful to Catherine, for she has deeply influenced my prayer and living. It is only fitting that someone who plumbed the mysteries of God with such depth was proclaimed a doctor of the church in 1970.

I am grateful to Suzanne Noffke, OP, for her assistance in helping me secure translations for many of the texts; to Sister Mary Jeremiah, who translated some needed passages of Catherine's letters over the phone; to Father David Sahatini of Sudan, Africa, who accompanied me to Siena, serving as my interpreter; and to Robert Smith, FSC, and Keith Egan, who have served as catalysts for this book. Last but certainly not least, I would like to thank God for everything contained herein.

PATRICIA MARY VINJE
Feast of Mary, Mother of Jesus
1 January 1989

✧ Introduction ✧

The Life and Legend of Catherine of Siena

Catherine of Siena wrote scores of letters to popes and nobles, monks and merchants. She told Pope Gregory to be a "manly man" and return the papacy to Rome. In a letter to Sir John Hawkwood, an English soldier-of-fortune, she pleaded with him to join a crusade to the Holy Land instead of stirring up trouble in Italy. Catherine accompanied a notorious criminal to the moment of his beheading. She nursed victims ravaged by the plague. Assassins tried to kill her as she arbitrated a dispute between the pope and the citizens of Florence. Mystic, peacemaker, theologian, preacher, nurse, and doctor of the church—all these titles apply to this unschooled woman who lived only thirty-three years.

The story of Catherine of Siena is an example of a kind of biography called *hagiography*, which is the study of people who serve as role models or as figures of inspiration, more to be admired than imitated. The term comes from two Greek words: *hagios* meaning "holy" and *graphos* meaning "writings." Thus, Catherine's biographers show her in only the best light, and the legends about her are embellished to inspire the reader to piety. Some of the stories about her—and even the passionate and image-filled language she employed—may strike people of the twentieth century as odd, if not neurotic. In the fourteenth century, however, talking of visions, expressing passionate love for God, and living solely to pray and serve other people were better understood, admired, and seen as signs of true holiness. So try to be open to Catherine by putting yourself into the images and simple faith of the fourteenth century.

Catherine's life and teaching present practical instruction for people of any age who are serious about their relationship with God, "the holy." The legends about Catherine comprise a key part of this teaching. The impact she left on her followers plays a significant role in our understanding of Catherine, not to mention its influence on the initial decision to preserve her texts. Both the oral and written tradition about Catherine work together to present a picture of this influential, fourteenth-century woman.

The Early Years

In the year 1347, Catherine Benincasa was born in Siena, Italy. She was the twenty-fourth child of Giacomo and Lapa Benincasa. Her father Giacomo had a dye shop on the first floor of the family home. The Fontebranda, a huge fountain supplying water to the area, was just around the corner from Catherine's house. She grew up amid a bustle of activity.

Catherine often played with her brother Stephen, who was two years older, and she was particularly close to her married sister Buonaventura, who lived on the outskirts of town. According to legend, one night in 1352 when Stephen and Catherine were walking home from Buonaventura's, Catherine paused at the top of a hill. She looked left over the valley toward the Church of San Domenico and saw a vision of Jesus above the church. He wore gold vestments and a papal tiara and sat on a throne. The apostles Peter, Paul, and John the Evangelist stood beside him. Jesus looked directly at Catherine, approached her, and made the sign of the cross over her. Stephen had gone ahead down the hill until he realized that Catherine was not with him. He called to her, but she remained transfixed, gazing at the vision above the church. Finally, Stephen caught her attention, and she turned briefly. When she looked back toward the vision, it had vanished. She burst into tears, wondering why she had looked away, for even a moment.

The experience profoundly affected this six-year-old girl, but she did not tell her family about what had happened. Catherine still played with the other children, but she now persuaded them to play "holy hermit" and taught them the Our Father and the Hail Mary.

According to her biographers, a year later Catherine saw a vision of Mary and Jesus. Mary presented Catherine to her son, and Catherine considered this a sign that she should consecrate herself solely to Jesus.

Catherine did not attend school. Girls were not taught to read in the fourteenth century. Nevertheless, Catherine went to church and studied the stained-glass windows and the statues in order to find out about the saints. She listened to the prayers at church and the sermons at Mass, learning how the saints proved their love for God by accepting insults, torture, and death. An orphaned cousin, Tommaso della Fonte, lived in the Benincasa house while studying for the priesthood. He read *The Golden Legend*, a collection of stories about the saints, to the whole family. Catherine listened avidly to these stories. Her family evidently remained unaware of her visions and her vow to God.

Catherine's Commitment Is Tested

When Catherine turned twelve, her family forbade her to walk the streets alone to attend daily Mass. She was old enough to marry, and social custom dictated this kind of seclusion until a suitable husband could be found for her.

At first Catherine resisted the family pressure to socialize, but then for a brief period she compromised and went to festivals with her family. Soon her brothers found a suitable bachelor for her. Catherine knew that she could not carry on the charade much longer, so she announced her commitment to Jesus and her refusal to marry anyone, ever. Her family enlisted the newly ordained cousin, Tommaso, to dissuade her. Instead, he supported Catherine and suggested that she cut off all her hair to prove her determination.

The family took severe measures with Catherine. They dismissed the kitchenmaid and gave Catherine all her duties as well as the scrubbing and the laundry. In addition, they forbade Catherine to be alone where she could think of God.

Distressed at first, Catherine turned this change of life-style to her advantage. She made a prayer space in her heart that she would never have to leave. She found a way to be in touch with God while she did the laundry and the cooking.

One day her father observed Catherine praying instead of attending to her work. Suddenly a white dove appeared over Catherine's head. At this sign, Catherine's father decided to help Catherine keep her vow to God. He told her brothers to stop looking for a husband for her, hired a servant to do the domestic work, and gave Catherine's room back to her so that she could pray in privacy.

Suffering with Jesus

Thirteen years old and unable to read, Catherine meditated on what was available to her—the little crucifix on the wall of her room. She experienced God's love for her flowing from the crucifix. To show her love for God in return, she followed the example of her contemporaries who used voluntary pain. She scourged herself three times a day, offering the pain for her sins and for the sins of everyone living or dead. She fasted and gave alms. Such self-imposed suffering may strike us as strange, but the kind of practices Catherine chose were considered normal for people in her time who were serious about living a holy life.

The roots of the fourteenth-century's cult of suffering reach back to the fourth century, when Christianity was legalized by Constantine. In the absence of martyrdom, certain individuals had decided to die in small ways for God, as if to say, "Instead of taking this meal, I will hand over this tiny pleasure of life to God. The money I do not spend on food, I will give to a hungry family. My appetite for pleasure will die a little bit today and a little bit tomorrow." Not everyone in the fourteenth century agreed with this notion of suffering. Catherine's mother, Lapa, coaxed her to go easier on herself.

Penance and prayer were not the only things that shaped Catherine's life. Catherine knew that accepting the unavoidable sufferings in life, the things over which she had no control, demanded far greater love. Numerous stories in Catherine's biographies show how she and her mother, both strong personalities, sparred to get their own ways. The stories shade the facts to show Catherine doing everything to give herself to God, while they depict Lapa acting selfishly to restrain her daughter.

Catherine's biographers, Raymond of Capua and Tommaso Caffarini, used Lapa as a foil the same way John the Evangelist used the Pharisees and Sadducees to provide an opportunity for Jesus to make a point. In Catherine's case, all her biographers depicted her fighting to live as a bride of Christ. They used Catherine's confrontations with her mother to illustrate Catherine's unshakable will. The more struggles Catherine endured, the stronger she appeared.

On the other hand, the saints and mystics realized that much of their struggle with evil was a struggle with their own inner demons as well as with outside forces and people. Catherine's writings reflect her recognition of such an inner struggle.

Catherine certainly relied on external means to help her cope with her inner struggles. She asked for the black-and-white Dominican habit, which she received at the age of eighteen. Although she belonged to the lay order of Dominican Mantellate, Catherine pronounced vows and practiced the life of the cloister in her room. In order to turn her full attention to God, she spoke only in confession, and she left her room only to attend Mass. She continued her regular schedule of prayer, fasting, and penances. Catherine realized the importance of the cross in her life. Suffering was inevitable, but if she wanted to imitate Jesus, some of this suffering must be taken on willingly.

Her Public Ministry

As her life of solitude in the little room continued, Catherine wanted to read in order to learn more about God. Frustrated with trying to teach herself to read, she pleaded with God to help her. She soon began to read fluently, although she still could not write. The ability to read changed her prayer because she could now recite the Divine Office.

She lived in solitude for three years. Then on Shrove Tuesday in 1367, her life took another turn. In a vision, Jesus united himself to her in mystical marriage. Before long Catherine felt called to leave the solitude of her cell to share what she had learned there and to serve the poor and sick people of Siena.

During this time of transition, Catherine began to eat with her family. After so much isolation, she felt somewhat awkward in the company of other people. Her former confessor, Tommaso della Fonte, visited her house and brought along other Dominicans like Tommaso Caffarini, a scholar who taught at the University of Siena, and Father Bartolomeo Dominic, who became her confessor. Catherine's earliest teachings were recorded during these conversations with visitors.

With other Mantellate, or Dominican laywomen, Catherine tended terminally ill patients at the La Scala Hospital. Many legends of Catherine's generous work evolved around her hospital activities.

During the summer of 1368, a wave of changes overtook the Benincasa household. Papa Giacomo died. A new political faction seized control of Siena and, as a result, the lives of Catherine's brothers became endangered. One night her brothers decided to seek refuge elsewhere because the whole family would be in peril if they stayed at home. Catherine escorted her brothers to La Scala Hospital. A hostile crowd threatened to attack the Benincasa men but pulled back at the sight of Catherine.

Soon after this incident Catherine, while visiting a friend, heard screams outside the window. Criminals were being carted to their execution. Told that they were not prepared for death, Catherine soon began ministering to the imprisoned, even accompanying the notorious Andrea de Bellanti to the gallows.

Spiritual Guide and Powerful Preacher

At twenty-four years of age, Catherine lacked formal education, yet scholarly men accepted her spiritual direction, calling her "Mother" or more affectionately "dearest Mama." Even her confessors accepted her counsel. Her company of followers included Dominican, Augustinian, and Franciscan friars, including Nero di Landoccio Pagliaresi, Stefano di Corrado Maconi, and Barduccio di Piero Canigiani. These men wrote letters for her and eventually took dictation for her book *The Dialogue*.

Catherine had women friends among the Mantellate, but many of them disapproved of men's treating her as an equal. The fact that a woman held conversations with men and appeared in public so often fostered rumors.

In the spring of 1374, the Dominican general chapter in Florence summoned Catherine to address accusations against her. She was not censured, as many had hoped she would be.

In fact, the Father General sent the well-known Dominican scholar, Raymond of Capua, to Siena to be her confessor and spiritual director. Raymond's affiliation with Catherine gave her greater credibility, not only in Siena, but in a wider church circle.

While Catherine was in Florence, the Black Death hit Siena, killing one-third of its population before the end of the summer of 1374. Upon her return to Siena, Catherine tended the sick.

In the following year, with Raymond's approval and encouragement, Catherine began preaching a message of repentance. Raymond accompanied her to the regions of Tuscany and Lombardy, serving as her private chaplain and hearing the confessions of numerous converts. Eventually more priests had to join the tours to help hear confessions and baptize converts. While Catherine was preaching in Pisa, so many people came to the church to hear her that penitents lined up outside the church and past the city gates. She also encouraged the Pisans to take part in a crusade to the Holy Land, and she attempted to persuade Pisa and Lucca to decline membership in the group of city-states that opposed the pope.

While Catherine was in Pisa praying before the crucifix in the Church of Santa Cristina, Jesus spoke to her from the cross. Her biographers record that the wounds of Christ were impressed upon her hands and feet. Henceforth, she shared more intimately in the sufferings of Jesus.

During the summer she returned to Siena in time to prepare the prisoner, Niccolo di Tuldo, to die. She knelt at his side at his beheading.

Peacemaker and Reformer

In the meantime, a French pope ruled the church from the royal palaces of Avignon, France, instead of residing in Rome. Due to political squabbles between the Italians and the French, the pope put the city of Florence under an interdict, meaning that no sacraments could be administered within the city limits, and no commerce could be transacted between Florentines and people from other cities, under penalty of excommunication for the parties involved.

In 1376, Catherine volunteered to speak to Pope Gregory XI on Florence's behalf. She traveled to Avignon to meet the pope and ask for the city's release from interdict. While in Avignon, she also talked to him about preaching a crusade and reforming the church, but corruption permeated the papal palaces in France. While Catherine's efforts on behalf of the Florentines were subverted and the interdict remained in force, she did manage to strengthen Pope Gregory's resolve to return to Rome. The following year he re-established the papacy there. Gregory died shortly afterward.

Catherine returned to Siena and founded a monastery of cloistered Dominican Sisters at the fortress at Belcaro. Raymond was restationed in Rome. In the midst of her activity, Catherine began having a series of mystical experiences that prompted her to begin her book *The Dialogue*. Evidently she learned to write at this time, but most of the book was dictated to secretaries.

Trouble began to brew between Florence and the new pope, Urban VI, who sent Catherine back to Florence to mediate. She negotiated with the townsfolk during the day but continued dictating her book in the evenings. Violence flared constantly in the city, and on 18 June 1378, an assassin tried to take Catherine's life. In a letter to Raymond, she expressed disappointment at not being a martyr. By August, Florence was released from the interdict. Catherine returned to Siena and completed her book in October.

A cabal of schismatic cardinals, displeased with the election of Urban to the pontificate, elected a rival pope named Clement VII, thereby instigating the Great Western Schism. As a reaction to Clement's election, Urban called Catherine to Rome in order to support his claim to the papacy. Catherine responded by moving to Rome with a group of her followers, where she remained until her death.

Pope Urban asked Catherine to address the papal curia in his support. Catherine was not as politically astute as legends suggest, but she had moral authority based on doing God's will and following the dictates of her conscience. If Catherine believed that something needed saying or doing, she said it or did it. Determining the effectiveness of her calls for reform is difficult. Corruption in the papal court and the schism in the church continued long after her death. Yet one tangible outcome of Catherine's years in Rome was a book of prayers that she wrote during this time.

At the beginning of 1380, Catherine became increasingly ill. She could not eat or drink. Even so, she daily walked to Saint Peter's for Mass and spent the entire day there praying for church unity and reform. On 26 February, she became paralyzed. Her friends thought that she would die immediately, but Catherine offered to suffer for the conversion of the church. She lingered for two months.

In April, friends overheard her praying that God would take her heart and use it for the church. Then God showed her a vision in which he took her heart and blessed the church with her blood. She thanked God for letting her take part in the struggle for unity and healing, and declared, "The victory is ours." On 29 April 1380, she exclaimed, "Into your hands I entrust my spirit," and died.

Catherine's Spirituality

Catherine's active life and her mystical experience cannot actually be separated. What she experienced in her prayer led her to reach out to sick and sinful people, to arbitrate disputes, and to seek reform in the church. Her daily activities were present in her prayer, and at the same time her prayer and contemplation were present in her activities to the extent that she often prayed in the middle of what she was doing or saying.

Catherine experienced the reality that union with God affects every fiber of our being and every action of our life. Episodes in Catherine's life and in our own lives are vessels that contain the presence and actions of God. The stuff of life is the meeting ground between humanity and divinity. The Scriptures bear out this truth time and again. Hearing the legend of Catherine is like entering into her spirit, which is a spirit wrapped in God and knit to the world.

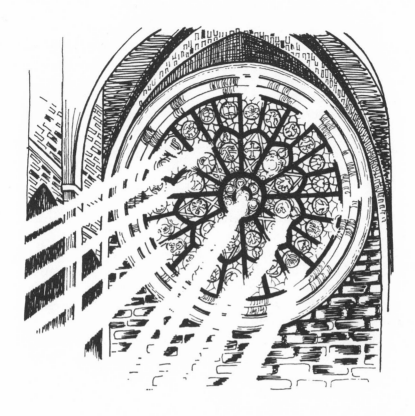

Whether one relies on the images in her visions or on the anecdotes from her life, the focus of attention never remains with the images as such. Mystics use images as means to describe an experience that is indescribable. The experience behind the images or words is what Catherine is truly attempting to convey. When we read Catherine's words, we need to be aware of the mystical experiences that impelled her to, for example, spend time with men on death row and to seek unity in the church.

Not only did her visions shape her life, but her life shaped her visions. Her images for describing God and the church come from landmarks in her hometown. The image of the fountain with which she described God resembles the Fontebranda fountain located near her house. This fountain is an underground river, rising to the surface just briefly at Siena.

Catherine's image of the bridge between heaven and earth resembles Florence's Ponte Vecchio bridge stretching over the Arno River. This wide bridge featured numerous shops on both sides of the walkway and a roof overhead.

Catherine's image of the blood of Jesus was probably rooted in the depiction of Christ's passion found in church windows and crucifixes. Also, the horrors of the Black Death and the dying patients she tended in the hospital possibly contributed to the development of this theme.

Catherine's Theology

The way Catherine expresses her understanding of God is as important as the facts she tells. One help to someone reading Catherine's words is to pay attention to the way she keeps repeating herself. Saint Paul was one of the earliest Christian writers to systematically use repetition, or recapitulation, for the sake of effect. When Paul repeated a point, he expanded it. New points that Paul made hooked onto everything else that had already been said about a given theme. For example:

✦ To love includes suffering.
✦ To love includes suffering and self-forgetfulness.
✦ To love one's neighbor includes suffering, self-forgetfulness, and compassion.
✦ To love will include suffering but one will not mind such suffering because such love already includes a self-forgetfulness.

Each repetition contained all the previous points in their entirety with a new teaching added.

Catherine wove together several motifs in her texts. The result of this is seen in *The Dialogue*, which is like a fabric carefully interwoven from several distinguishable threads. Such recapitulation mirrors life. Everyday life is full of scenes that keep repeating themselves.

Catherine's use of images fits well into her circular, repetitive method of explaining her experience of God. Images often carry a number of meanings, on a number of levels, simultaneously. Catherine gave layers of meaning to images such as the cell, the bridge, and the fountain. She repeated these images. Every time she used an image, she tended to include all that she had previously said about that image before presenting new meanings for that symbol. In this way, she developed the theological meaning of her experience.

Major Themes:
Truth, Obedience, Love, and the Trinity

In Catherine's spirituality, the interplay between themes like truth and obedience, or knowledge and love, is constant. For example, love led her to the truth that God is in everyone, and this caused her to love everyone. Four themes seem to be particularly dominant in Catherine's spirituality: truth, obedience to God's will, love, and the Trinity.

Truth. Catherine took the Dominican motto, "Veritas," or truth, as her own. She considered truth, which she also called humility, to be the root of spiritual life.

Obedience to God's Will. But if truth is the foundation of her theology, what is its culmination? Referring once again to the Dominican heritage and in particular to its rule and constitution, obedience to God's will is essential in Catherine's teaching. In fact, Dominicans take only the vow of obedience. By obeying God's will, a person imitates Jesus, who emptied himself first of divinity and then of humanity in order to express his love to the Creator and all creatures.

The Dominican charisms of truth and obedience are scriptural themes. John's gospel and Paul's epistles are two of the major sources of these themes, which are emphasized in Dominican spirituality.

Love. Truth and obedience are faces of love. Love, truth, and obedience form a triad of virtues reflecting the Trinity. Love creates. Truth is the wisdom that came to earth clothed in flesh. Obedience to God's will in the heart of Jesus and in the heart of all creatures indicates the presence of the Spirit.

The Trinity. The content of Catherine's theology is Trinitarian. Catherine provides numerous repetitions of the threefold manifestation of God and the threefold reflection of God in creatures. She develops the themes of the power, the wisdom, and the love of God to describe the Father, the Son, and the Spirit. She uses the human attributes of remembering, understanding, and desiring in order to describe how human activity reflects divine operations. She shows that being nourished by Christ in the Eucharist and then reaching out to one's neighbor in love are acts of love flowing from the Trinity.

Catherine's Trinitarian theology draws on the Scriptures. The Scriptures are normative for all Christian teaching. Catherine understood the central core of teaching embodied in the Scriptures: To live with God and in God and in union with others, "To love and be loved."

Catherine's prayers, teaching, and experience magnify God's immense love for every individual. She does not separate her ideas from one another, and she does not separate her prayer from her ideas, nor does she isolate her works of charity or her friends from her passionate longing for God. All the components of her life and teaching flow in and out of each other, in union with the joyful interplay of the Creator, the Son, and the Spirit.

How to Pray with Catherine

Sometimes the words *meditation* and *contemplation* are used interchangeably, but there is difference between the two.

Meditation is one of the steps to contemplation. There are different ways of talking about the approach to prayer, but borrowing a four-step method of prayer that was developed in the early church and later revived in the monasteries of the Middle Ages can be helpful in praying with Catherine.

1. According to this format, in the first stage of prayer we listen to something read about God, or we look at a stained-glass window, studying the details in order to learn about the "things of God." This first step is called *lectio*, which means "reading."

2. The second step entails thinking about the reading or picture. This thinking is called *meditatio*.

3. In the third step, *oratio*, or "praying," we stop "thinking about" God and begin "talking to" God.
4. The fourth step is *contemplatio*. In this stage we stop talking to God and begin feasting on God or tasting God. For the sake of clarity, one might say that meditation is similar to thinking about an ice cream cone, and contemplation is like actually eating the ice cream. An important part of tasting God is to be with God often during the day.

If you feel a movement in your heart leading you into God during your prayer time, you need not finish the reflections in a meditation. Follow God's lead.

Sit quietly, kneel down, stand expectantly, pause, dance, walk, or bow down. The incidentals do not matter: "For Yahweh will take delight in you" (Isaiah 62:4).

On your spiritual journey, your companion, Catherine, would encourage you:

Be still!

Look on your God, loving you.

✧ Meditation 1 ✧

Putting on Truth

Theme: Catherine continually prayed to be clothed with eternal truth.

Opening prayer: May I come before the truth and have the courage to be honest in facing myself and the situations of life. May I come before the face of God, and bring all that is hidden into the light.

About Catherine

During her lifetime, Catherine often faced people who challenged her honesty, virtue, and wisdom. In one such instance, Brother Gabriele, a Franciscan scholar, and Brother Giovanni, an Augustinian, tried to trap Catherine. But she saw through them and, forcing them to face the truth, brought them to conversion.

These two able regular priests and scholars often talked with each other and murmured against that blessed maiden Catherine, saying: "This ignorant little woman seduces the simple and ignorant with her false interpretations of Holy Scripture, and thus leads many souls with her to hell. May it not be our duty to speak to her so that she may see her errors?"

. . . The two theologians decided to visit Catherine. As it happened, a large number of the circle were assembled. . . . The Franciscan and Augustinian now stepped into the midst of this circle and having found seats, began to examine Catherine and subject her to a series of questions, each more captious than the last.

Now Master Gabriele lived in his convent in the style of a cardinal. He had had the walls taken down between three cells to make himself a spacious room; his bed was provided with curtains and rugs of silk; he possessed books and many other things worth many hundred ducats. Catherine knew this and suddenly she upset all the snares which the Franciscan had prepared for her and told him to be ashamed of the life that he, a son of Saint Francis, dared to live. "How is it possible for you to understand anything of that which pertains to the kingdom of God," she exclaimed, "you who live only for the world and to be honoured and esteemed by men? Your learning is of but little use to others and only harms yourself, for you seek the shell, not the core. For the sake of Jesus Christ Crucified, do not live on this way any longer!" Her exhortation was so forcible that the learned Franciscan took the keys from his belt and handed them to Catherine, saying: "Is there no one present here who will go to my cell and take everything he finds there and give it to the poor?"

. . . The learned man changed his mode of life to such an extent that soon after he went to Florence and humbly served at table as a lay brother in the convent of Santa Croce. Master Giovanni Tantucci too, gave away all his possessions. (Jorgensen, *Saint Catherine*, pp. 145–146)

Pause: Reflect on how, in challenging others, we sometimes call them to the truth about themselves.

Catherine's Words

Catherine knew that the experience of truth has an impact on a person's entire being. In *The Dialogue*, she records God telling her:

> Paul [the apostle], then, had seen and tasted this when I drew him up to the third heaven, to the height of the Trinity. He tasted and knew my Truth, for there he received the Holy Spirit in his fullness and learned the teaching of my Truth, the incarnate Word. Paul's soul was clothed in me, the eternal Father, through feeling and union, just as the blessed are in everlasting life. His soul, though, had not left his body, but the feeling and union were there. But it pleased my goodness to make of him a chosen vessel in the very depths of me, the eternal Trinity. Therefore I stripped him of myself, since no suffering can befall me, and I wanted him to suffer for my name. Then I put before his mind's eye Christ crucified. I clothed him in the garment of his teaching and bound and chained him with the mercy of the Holy Spirit, the fire of charity. He was like a ready vessel, remade by my goodness, for he put up no resistance when he was struck. No, he said, "My Lord, what do you want me to do? Tell me what you want me to do and I will do it." I taught him when I set Christ crucified before his eye and clothed him in my Truth's teaching. Once most perfectly enlightened by the light of true contrition grounded in my charity, through which he repented of his sin, he clothed himself in the teaching of Christ crucified. And he so held on to it (as he revealed to you) that he was never stripped of it. (Pp. 152–153)

Reflection

Catherine sought the Truth: God, who is love and who has gifted us in wonderful ways.

Facing and accepting the truth about ourselves and realizing our status in God's eyes is humility. In the presence of the Holy One, we may feel like Ezekiel, who fell on his face until God said, "Get to your feet; I will speak to you" (Ezekiel 2:1b).

God wants us to stand up and face our blessedness and sinfulness. In embracing our humanity, we realize our need for God
and understand the nature of God's gifts to us. Facing and accepting truth enabled Catherine and enables us to challenge
the deceptions in the world around us.

✧ Pray repeatedly Catherine's words, "My Lord, what
do you want me to do? I will do it," or these words from John
8:32, "The truth will set you free." Use one of these as a prayer
when you are confused or tempted to deceive.

✧ We hate in others what we most fear in ourselves.
Think about two or three people with whom you regularly
find yourself in conflict—people whom you sometimes hate.
What is it about them that you most dislike? Then, ask yourself what you hate in them that you most fear in yourself. Ask
the Spirit of Truth to be with you in your meditation. Ask
Jesus to reform your perception of these other people.

✧ Deception is subtle in our lives. We can deceive ourselves for quite a long time without being aware of it. Examine
your consciousness. Looking at the last several days, can you
name any instances during which you deceived yourself or
hid the truth from yourself or others? Is there any one thing
that you do not want to face about yourself? Remember that
Jesus is with you. Dialog with him about why you hold on to
this untruth. Ask Jesus how you would be better off facing the
truth. Petition him for the courage to be truthful.

✧ Write a list of your gifts and talents as a litany of
thanksgiving: for example, "For the gift of my gentleness with
children, thank you loving God." Pray your litany slowly,
offering thanks to God for your gifts.

✧ In "About Catherine" we see her confronting the
hypocrisy of her two accusers. In doing so, she helped them
reform their lives. Draw up a list of deceptive practices
commonly employed by advertisers, agencies, companies, or

individuals. Are there ways in which you can confront these people to call them to truth and reform? Converse with Jesus about how you can be a truth-bringer.

God's Word

So they said to him, "Who are you?" Jesus answered:
    What I have told you from the outset.
    About you I have much to say
    and much to judge;
    but the one who sent me is true,

and what I declare to the world
I have learnt from him. . . .
To the Jews who believed in him Jesus said:
If you make my word your home
you will indeed be my disciples;
you will come to know the truth
and the truth will set you free.
They answered, "We are descended from Abraham and
we have never been the slaves of anyone; what do you
mean, 'You will be set free?'" Jesus replied:
In all truth I tell you,
everyone who commits sin is a slave.
Now a slave has no permanent standing in the
household,
but a son belongs to it forever.
So if the Son sets you free,
you will indeed be free.

(John 8:25–26,31–36)

Closing Prayer: Conclude your meditation with these
words from Catherine's *Prayers* (p. 105):

O eternal Trinity,
my sweet love!
You, light,
give us light.
You, wisdom,
give us wisdom.
You, supreme strength,
strengthen us.
Today, eternal God,
let our cloud be dissipated
so that we may perfectly know and follow your truth,
in truth,
with a free and simple heart.

✧ **Meditation 2** ✧

The Trinity: Deep Well of Love

Theme: God's love is like a deep well flowing with purest water that nurtures and satisfies each creature.

Opening prayer: Let us pray to know our God intimately and to be drawn into life wholeheartedly by this love.

About Catherine

Catherine consoled and prepared for death several men who were condemned to die. The government of Siena readily meted out the death penalty for any criticism. A young man, Niccolo di Tuldo, made some remarks against the ruling regime while he was drinking. Arrested, convicted, and condemned to die, the young man despaired, declaring that a God who allowed his death for such a small offense could not be good and just.

Catherine went to visit him. Niccolo calmed down, made his confession, and received communion for the first time. In the midst of their meeting, Niccolo asked Catherine to be with him at the moment of his death. She kept her promise, escorting him to the place of execution. Catherine tells that he smiled at her, saying "Jesus" and "Caterina." She caressed his head as he laid it on the block. Just at the moment of execution, Catherine had this vision:

> Then one saw the God-and-man as one sees the splendor of the Sun. He was open and received . . . the soul which he put in the open treasure house, [of] his side, full of mercy revealing that the first Truth received him by grace and mercy alone, and for no other reason. . . .
>
> Thus, [Niccolo's soul] was received by God through power and the Son, wisdom word Incarnate gave him and made him share in the crucified love with which [Christ] accepted his painful and shameful death in obedience to the Father for the good of the human race; and the hands of the Holy Spirit locked him within.
>
> He made a gesture sweet enough to draw a thousand hearts. And I do not wonder because he already tasted the divine sweetness. He turned as the bride does when she has reached the threshold of her spouse, and turns her head around and looks, bowing to those who accompanied her, and with a gesture shows a sign of thanks. (Letter T273, unpublished translation by Sister Mary Jeremiah Gillett)

Splashed with blood, Catherine refrained from washing her habit, knowing that Niccolo's blood was proof of his being embraced by God.

Pause: Reflect on God's love and forgiveness.

Catherine's Words

In *The Dialogue,* Catherine records that "the high eternal Father" describes our relationship to the Trinity in this way:

> It was with providence that I created you, and when I contemplated my creature in myself I fell in love with the beauty of my creation. It pleased me to create you in my image and likeness with great providence. I provided you with the gift of memory so that you might hold fast my benefits and be made a sharer in my own, the eternal Father's power. I gave you understanding so that in the wisdom of my only-begotten Son you might comprehend

and know what I the eternal Father want, I who gave you graces with such burning love. I gave you a will to love, making you a sharer in the Holy Spirit's mercy, so that you might love what your understanding sees and knows.

All this my gentle providence did, only that you might be capable of understanding and enjoying me and rejoicing in my goodness by seeing me eternally. (P. 277)

Reflection

The Trinity is one. The figures of the Creator, the Son, and the Spirit present a dynamic relationship sometimes called the "round dance" of love—a joyful, loving reverence, an interplay of persons.

Catherine showed the love of God to Niccolo di Tuldo, the same love that she experienced so profoundly. All of us are made in order to rejoice in God's love forever.

❖ To reinforce the message that God loves you, select one of the consoling phrases from "Catherine's Words" and pray it over and over again. Allow the words to heal your wounded spirit.

❖ What might be some signs that you are searching for the total love of God? Do you ever feel that things are not right or that something is missing in your life? Do you ever feel lonely? Do you ever feel lonely for God?

Be still in God's presence. Then ask God to be with you and to help you recall ways in which you have been shown God's love by your gifts and by other people.

❖ Love brings understanding. Recall, perhaps write about, an experience in which love helped you understand someone or something. Thank God, who is Love, for this understanding.

❖ If a troublesome thought—anxiety, anger, worry, resentment—comes to mind, thank God for allowing you to remember this hurt that you have been carrying. Perhaps God is reminding you of this hurt or confusion today so it can be healed and forgiven. If you did not recall such negative emotions, they would never be addressed and consequently never healed. Lift up this memory to God. Hand over the pain to God.

✧ Catherine shared God's love with Niccolo in his time of agony. As part of your prayer, call or visit persons who you know are suffering either physically, mentally, or spiritually. Be a loving presence to them. Or you might write to someone who is suffering and needs consolation and affirmation.

✧ If you have a favorite song that praises the loving God, why not sing it, whistle it, or play it on an instrument?

God's Word

This, then, is what I pray
kneeling before the Father,
from whom every fatherhood,
in heaven or on earth,
takes its name.
In the abundance of his glory may he,
through his Spirit,
enable you to grow firm in power
with regard to your inner self,
so that Christ may live
in your hearts through faith, and then,
planted in love and built on love,
with all God's holy people
you will have the strength to grasp
the breadth and the length,
the height and the depth; so that,
knowing the love of Christ,
which is beyond knowledge,
you may be filled with
the utter fullness of God.

(Ephesians 3:14–19)

Closing prayer: Complete your meditation with the following words from Catherine's *Prayers* (pp. 187–88):

We were enclosed,
O eternal Father,
within the garden of your bosom.
You drew us out of your holy mind
like a flower
petaled with our soul's three powers, . . .
You gave us memory
so that we might be able to hold your blessings
and so bring forth the flower of glory to your name
and the fruit of profit to ourselves.
You gave us understanding
to understand your truth
and your will—
your will that wants only that we be made holy—
so that we might bear first the flower of glory
and then the fruit of virtue.
And you gave us our will
so that we might be able to love
what our understanding has seen
and what our memory has held.

For this, we praise and thank you.
Amen.
Amen.
Amen.

✧ **Meditation 3** ✧

Loving One Another

Theme: Catherine put her love for other people into action, taking seriously Jesus' command to love her neighbors as she loved herself.

Opening prayer: I pray for a deep love among my brothers and sisters, a love that deepens in times of differences and difficulties as well as in times of joy and success.

About Catherine

Knowing that the surest means of pleasing the divine Spouse was to be charitable towards the neighbor, her heart burned with the desire of relieving him in all his wants. . . . She was acquainted with some poor families, in her neighborhood, who were in great distress, but who were ashamed to solicit alms. She therefore imitated Saint Nicholas, rising early in the morning, so as to carry corn, wine and oil, with whatever else was necessary for them. . . . One day as she was sick and suffering from head to foot, and felt it was impossible for her to rise from her bed, she learned that a poor widow in the neighborhood was in absolute destitution, having not even a loaf of bread for her little children. Her heart bled, and during the whole night she was begging her divine Spouse to render her sufficient corporal strength to go to the relief of this unhappy woman. She arose before daylight, ran over the house, filled a little sack with meal, took a large bottle of wine, a jug of oil, all the aliments that she could find prepared. (Raymond, *Saint Catharine*, 1960, pp. 83–85)

Pause: Reflect on the ways in which you care for your neighbor.

Catherine's Words

I [God] ask you to love me with the same love with which I love you. But for me you cannot do this, for I loved you without being loved. Whatever love you have for me you owe me, so you love me not gratuitously but out of duty, while I love you not out of duty but gratuitously. So you cannot give me the kind of love I ask of you. This is why I have put you among your neighbors: so that you can do for them what you cannot do for me—that is, love them without any concern for thanks and without looking for any profit for yourself. And whatever you do for them I will consider done for me. (*The Dialogue*, p. 121)

Reflection

Catherine understood the power of redemptive love. The love that Jesus gives humankind is unmerited and undeserved. Our redemption and healing are pure gift. Jesus does not need what humans can give back, and so he told us to serve one another freely and generously out of love.

Jesus' love for us required self-sacrifice, ultimately death on the cross. Our love for other people calls for self-giving that may sometimes be inconvenient, unappreciated, and burdensome. However, the love of Jesus and other people for us may be inconvenient, unappreciated, and burdensome. Redemptive love affirms, heals, and saves us. The charity of Jesus manifests itself through our love.

✧ Reflect on times when people have cared for you and times when you have cared for other people. Write or recall the name of someone who gave you the gift of healing and the way in which you were healed, and then write down or recall the name of someone to whom you gave this same gift and what was required in the giving:

✦ *The gift of healing* (physical, emotional, or spiritual):
I received the gift from . . . when he or she . . .
I gave the gift to . . . when I . . .
✦ *The gift of feeding* (physical, emotional, or spiritual):
I received the gift from . . . when he or she . . .
I gave the gift to . . . when I . . .
✦ *The gift of sheltering* (physical, emotional, or spiritual):
I received the gift from . . . when he or she . . .
I gave the gift to . . . when I . . .
✦ *The gift of hospitality:*
I received the gift from . . . when he or she . . .
I gave the gift to . . . when I . . .
✦ *The gift of visiting:*
I received the gift from . . . when he or she . . .
I gave the gift to . . . when I . . .

After you have made your list of names and recalled the instances of love received and given, talk with Jesus about each person and ask Jesus how you could be a better lover of other people.

✧ One way of serving humankind is to cherish and care for creation. Consider two ways in which you have cared for the earth over the last two days. Then in dialog with the Holy Spirit, ponder two ways in which you could show more care for the earth.

✧ Catherine had to pray for Jesus' strength to help the needy widow. Bring to mind some situation in which you find love very difficult to give or some person who is hard to love. Spend time with Jesus, asking for the courage and strength to give love in this situation or to this person.

✧ During this day or for several days, use this short prayer to remind yourself to love: "Whatever you do for them, I will consider done for me."

God's Word

When the Son of man comes in his glory, escorted by all
the angels, then he will take his seat on his throne of glory. All nations will be assembled before him and he will
separate people one from another as the shepherd sepa-
rates sheep from goats. He will place the sheep on his
right hand and the goats on his left. Then the King will
say to those on his right hand, "Come, you whom my Father has blessed, take as your heritage the kingdom prepared for you since the foundation of the world. For I was
hungry and you gave me food, I was thirsty and you gave
me drink, I was a stranger and you made me welcome,
lacking clothes and you clothed me, sick and you visited
me, in prison and you came to see me. Then the upright

will say to him in reply, "Lord, when did we see you hungry and feed you, or thirsty and give you drink? When did we see you a stranger and make you welcome, lacking clothes and clothe you? When did we find you sick or in prison and go to see you?" And the King will answer, "In truth I tell you, in so far as you did this to one of the least of these brothers of mine, you did it to me." (Matthew 25:31–40)

Closing prayer: God, teach us to love the people in our midst, and in doing so, to love the God in our midst.

✦ **Meditation 4** ✦

The Cell of
Self-Knowledge

Theme: Under divine inspiration, Catherine built a cell—a private room—within her heart to which she could always return to be with God.

Opening prayer: May I gain a deep knowledge of myself and of you, God of all wisdom.

About Catherine

Catherine's family insisted on arranging a prospective husband for her, but Catherine had consecrated herself to God alone. To discourage her family's efforts, Catherine cut off her hair. Considering this as an affront, her family took away her tiny, private room so that she could not pray so much. They dismissed the kitchenmaid and gave all of her work to Catherine. Rather than be upset by her family's behavior, Catherine was inspired to enter into the cell of her heart.

> The result was that she who formerly had been sometimes inside and sometimes outside the walls of that material cell which she then possessed, now remained uninterruptedly within the walls of that inner cell of the heart which no one could take from her. (Raymond, *Catherine of Siena*, pp. 46–47)

Pause: Reflect on the presence of a private cell in your own heart.

Catherine's Words

In a letter to her first confessor, Tommaso della Fonte, Catherine describes the cell within the heart:

> Dearest father, I beg you to fulfill my longing to see you united with and transformed in God. But this is impossible unless we are one with his will. *Oh sweetest eternal will, to have taught us how to discover your holy will!* If we were to ask that gentlest most loving young Man and most merciful Father, this is how he would answer us: "Dearest children, if you wish to discover and experience the effects of my will, dwell within the cell of your soul." This cell is a well in which there is earth as well as water. In the earth we can recognize our own poverty: we see that we are not. For we *are* not. We see that our being is from God. Oh ineffable blazing charity! I see next that as we discover the earth [i.e., our poverty] we get to the living water, the very core of the knowledge of his true and gentle will which desires nothing else but that we be made holy. So let us enter into the depths of that well; for if we dwell there, we will necessarily come to know both ourselves and God's goodness. In recognizing that we are nothing we humble ourselves. And in humbling ourselves we enter that flaming, consumed heart, opened up like a window without shutters, never to be closed. As we focus there the eye of the free will God has given us, we see and know that his will has become nothing other than our sanctification.
>
> *Love, sweet love! Open, open up our memory for us, so that we may receive, hold fast, and understand God's great goodness!* For as we understand, so we love, and when we love, we find ourselves united with the transformed in love, in this mother charity, having passed through and

yet ever passing through the gate that is Christ crucified. He said as much to his disciples: "I will come and make my dwelling place with you." (*Letters*, p. 44)

Reflection

As Catherine saw herself within God, she realized that the inner cell is the knowledge of God's intimate activity in our deepest center. Catherine believed in the need to go apart for a while to meet God in the depth of this cell. The notion of going off alone is a common theme in the gospels. Recall how many times Jesus went up a mountain or got into a boat to pray alone.

Catherine spent three years in solitude in her bedroom cell before she began serving the people of Siena. As she came to know God and herself better, Catherine regarded her inner cell as the home of God. The experience of the divine presence within her drew Catherine outward to others in compassion.

✧ Read "Catherine's Words" again, more slowly this time. Ponder phrases and pray them, that is, repeat them several times until you have savored their meaning, all the while offering these words to God as your own prayer.

✧ Visit or picture a place in nature that helps you feel the presence of God. To be aware of God's presence in this place, close your eyes and breathe deeply, inhaling and exhaling slowly. If you are at the place, open your eyes, ears, nose, and touch to all the sensations around you. Remember that all of creation is holy ground.

If you cannot go physically to this special place, relax with the deep breathing and then travel in your imagination to the place, the holy ground. Open your imagination's eyes, ears, nose, and touch to the sensations. Still yourself. Be present to nature and to God in the place in your heart, as if you were there in body. Bask in the wonder of the scene. Let God speak to you.

✧ Think of your body as the treasure it is. Slow down. Let the beating of your heart quiet down.

✦ Find a word or phrase that is meaningful to you. You might choose *Jesus; Come, Jesus; Peace;* or *Love.* Breathe in slowly and deeply. As you breathe in, pray the word or phrase.

✦ As you breathe out, imagine all the tension or sadness of the day leaving you. Feel sin leaving you. Breathe in the peace of Jesus, and breathe out whatever weighs you down. Gradually let go of the words you are saying and just breathe deeply. As you breathe in, enter the quiet of your own heart. Enter more and more deeply into your own heart. Rest in its stillness. Rest in the presence of God.

While you are in your inner cell, bring to mind the people you love. Just thinking of other people, slowly saying their names, is a way to bring them into the presence of God. You might want to say the name of Jesus and alternate this with the name of a loved one: "Jesus . . . Phil . . . Jesus . . . Liz . . . Jesus . . . "

✧ Recall one of the stories in the Scriptures where someone goes aside to pray. Imagine that you are with Elijah in a cave (I Kings 19:9–18) or with Mary Magdalene by the tomb in the garden (John 20:1–18) or with Jesus praying in the desert (Luke 5:16) or with Mary at the time the angel Gabriel visits her (Luke 1:26–38). In your imagination, picture this person's face. Walk inside the cave, or the tomb, or the house of Mary. This is a safe place where you can meet God. Smell the dampness of the cave, or the wind and sand of the desert. Listen to the quiet and let the quiet enter inside you. What does the Holy Spirit say to you in the silence?

✧ If you keep a journal, write down some of the thoughts that have come to you during your reflection.

God's Word

I am going now to prepare a place for you,
and after I have gone and prepared you a place,
I shall return to take you to myself,
so that you may be with me
where I am. . . .
I shall ask the Father,
and he will give you another Paraclete
to be with you for ever,
the Spirit of truth
whom the world can never accept
since it neither sees nor knows him;
but you know him,
because he is with you, he is in you.
I shall not leave you orphans; . . .

(John 14:2b–3,16–18)

Closing prayer: Close your meditation with these gentle words from Catherine's *Prayers* (pp. 186–88):

We were enclosed,
O eternal Father,
within the garden of your bosom.
You drew us out of your holy mind
like a flower

. . . .

so that we might bear fruit in your garden,
might come back to you

. . . .

There the soul dwells—
like the fish in the sea
and the sea in the fish.

✧ **Meditation 5** ✧

The River of Sin

Theme: Catherine pictured sin as "the flood of a stormy river that beat against [us] constantly with its waves, bringing weariness and troubles" (*The Dialogue*, p. 58). She knew that we would drown in sin, except for God's love.

Opening prayer: Grant me the grace to see my sinfulness and to know your tender mercy, loving God.

About Catherine

Raymond of Capua related how he was skeptical of all the reports he heard about Catherine's miracles and how he explored every avenue possible to find out whether her visions or miracles were from God or not. In prayer he asked for some unmistakable sign that her manner of life was inspired by the Holy Spirit. The following day Catherine came to speak to him. Raymond writes:

> She kept on speaking on the subject she had begun. And as she spoke my sins came before my mind with a clarity I had never before experienced. The veil was torn from my eyes, and I saw myself standing at the bar of my divine Judge, . . . but I saw, too, the kindness of that Judge and his tender mercy. . . . I burst out into such a torrent of tears and sobs as, I must reluctantly confess, made me

fear my very breast and heart would be ruptured. Catherine discreetly said not another word, as though this was the very purpose for which she had come. She let me have my cry and my fit of sobbing out to the end. . . . Then she rose to her feet, and I have the impression that, coming behind me, she lightly laid her hand upon my shoulders as she said, "Keep God's gifts in mind." (*Catherine of Siena*, pp. 81–82)

Pause: Ponder Catherine's advice to Raymond.

Catherine's Words

In her dialogs with God, Catherine records God's message to her:

First know your own weakness, how ready that perverse law bound up in your members makes you to rebel against me your Creator. Not that this law can force any one of you to commit the least sin unless you want to, but it certainly does fight against the spirit. Nor did I give this law so that my people should be conquered, but so that they might increase and prove virtue in their souls. For virtue can be proved only by its opposite. . . .

I gave the soul this law also to keep her truly humble. So you see, while I created her in my image and likeness and made her so honorable and beautiful, I gave her as well the vilest thing there is, this perverse law. In other words, I bound her into a body formed from the vilest earth so that when she saw her beauty she would not lift up her head in pride against me. So the weak body is a reason for humility to those who have this light [of mine]. They have no reason at all to be proud, but they do have reason for true and perfect humility. This perverse law, then, no matter how it fights, cannot force the least sin. Rather it is reason for you to learn to know yourself and to know how inconstant is the world. (*The Dialogue*, p. 185)

Reflection

One way to appreciate our goodness is to acknowledge our own weakness. The converse is also true. To know our own weakness requires recognition of our goodness.

❖ Meditate on all that is good in you. Name and list some of your good qualities. For instance:
✦ I have a wonderful smile.
✦ I listen to other people's points of view.
Try to list as many of your positive gifts as you can.
Form the good things you find in yourself into a litany. As you read through this list, thank or praise God for these good or happy qualities that you have and share. For example:
✦ With this gift of a smile, I praise you, God.
✦ For my ability to listen, I praise you, God.
Then go over this same list, as a litany of mercy, saying something like this:
✦ For the loss of laughter, mercy, Lord.
✦ For inattentiveness to other points of view, mercy, Lord.

❖ You may want to find a dark place for this activity.
1. Light a candle. Have a large aluminum pan or tin can ready.
2. On gray paper, write down an area of darkness in your life.
3. On white paper, write down a thing you can do to bring light into the world. (If you are alone you may want to use several pieces of paper for both categories. If you are in a group, one gray paper and one white paper per person will be enough.)
4. Collect all the gray papers and all the white papers. One at a time, burn the gray papers; every time a paper is lit, one of the white papers is read aloud.
As the gray papers burn in the offering dish, the room becomes brighter; as the good deeds are read off in the growing brightness, try to appreciate the sense of the darkness being overcome by light.

❖ Reflect on five times in your life that you have hurt people. If you still feel awkward or uneasy about any of these incidents, jot down the events or the names of the people.

Then select just one person or event. Tell Jesus how you feel about the event. Be honest and show all the anger to Jesus so that your entire hurt can be healed. You would not hurt someone else unless you were already hurting. As you express your anger, try to express just how hurt you feel underneath the anger.

What other pressures were you reacting to when you hurt that person? You were not only reacting to that person, but also to all the other pressures in your life. Can you forgive yourself for reacting to internal and external pressures?

Have some good results occurred because of the hurt? This can include ways you grew and ways the other person grew. Are you more honest with yourself? Are you more honest with the other person? Is there a practical way for you to pick up and begin again with the person you have hurt? Consider ways in which you can be reconciled.

God's Word

Yahweh, you search me and know me.
You know if I am standing or sitting.
You perceive my thoughts from far away.
Whether I walk or lie down, you are watching;
you are familiar with all my ways.
Before a word is even on my tongue, Yahweh,
you know it completely.

. . . .

Where could I go to escape your spirit?
Where could I flee from your presence?

. . . .

If I flew to the point of sunrise—
or far across the sea—
your hand would still be guiding me,
your right hand holding me.

. . . .

You created my inmost being
and knit me together in my mother's womb.
For all these mysteries—
for the wonder of myself,
for the wonder of your works—
I thank you.

. . . .

God, search me and know my heart;
probe me and know my thoughts.
Make sure I do not follow evil ways,
and guide me in the way of life eternal.

(Psalm 139)

Closing prayer: Conclude your meditation with these words from Catherine's *Prayers* (p. 114):

Grant, most gracious Father,
your sweet eternal benediction,
and in the blood of your Son
wash the face of our souls. Amen.

✧ Meditation 6 ✧

Crossing the Bridge

Theme: To Catherine, Jesus is the bridge on which we can cross over the many stormy seas of life without drowning.

Opening prayer: O Triune God, help me to cross the bridge by climbing onto the feet of Jesus, then help me enter into the heart of Jesus. Be with me as I approach the mouth of Jesus, expecting mercy.

About Catherine

Tommaso della Fonte, Catherine's first confessor, was in Pisa with her for most of her preaching campaign. Catherine stayed in Pisa when the mission ended in order to discourage the townspeople from affiliating with the antipapal league of Milan and Florence. Tommaso preceded her to Siena. Catherine's efforts at mediation in the political arena were not warmly accepted. Her approach to the criticism and danger that she and Tommaso were in is indicated in a letter to Tommaso in 1375:

> I, Catherine, a useless servant and your unworthy daughter, commend myself to you in the precious blood of God's Son. How I long to see you slaughtered on the tree of the sweet beloved cross—but not without me! I see no other refreshment for us, dearest father, but to agonize up there in blazing love. There will be no demons, seen or

unseen, who can take from us the life of grace, because once we are lifted up, earth will not be able to get in our way. As the mouth of Truth said, "If I am lifted up I will draw everything to myself"—for he draws heart and soul and will with all his strength.

So, dearest father, let's make the cross our bed—for I am jubilantly happy with your message. To think the world is opposing us! I don't deserve such mercy from them, that they should give me the cloak our sweet eternal Father wore. (*Letters*, pp. 143–144)

Pause: Reflect on Catherine's embrace of suffering, even death, for the sake of peace.

Catherine's Words

In one of their dialogs, God spoke these words to Catherine:

But first I want you to look at the bridge of my only-begotten Son, and notice its greatness. Look! It stretches from heaven to earth, joining the earth of your humanity with the greatness of the Godhead. This is what I mean when I say it stretches from heaven to earth—through my union with humanity.

This was necessary if I wanted to remake the road that had been broken up, so that you might pass over the bitterness of the world and reach life. From earth alone I could not have made it great enough to cross the river and bring you to eternal life. The earth of human nature by itself, as I have told you, was incapable of atoning for sin and draining off the pus from Adam's sin, for that stinking pus had infected the whole human race. Your nature had to be joined with the height of mine, the eternal Godhead, before it could make atonement for all of humanity. Then human nature could endure the suffering, and the divine nature, joined with that humanity, would accept my son's sacrifice on your behalf to release you from death and give you life.

So the height stooped to the earth of your humanity, bridging the chasm between us and rebuilding the road. And why should he have made of himself a roadway? So that you might in truth come to the same joy as the angels. But my Son's having made of himself a bridge for you could not bring you to life unless you make your way along that bridge. (*The Dialogue*, p. 59)

Reflection

Catherine sometimes called the bridge—Jesus—a ladder, and sometimes she called it the cross. She sought to imitate Jesus, who suffered and died, bridging the gap between humanity and divinity.

❖ Spend a period of time meditating about the cross. Imagine that you are standing in front of Jesus, dying on the cross. Jesus looks down into your eyes and says, "I draw you to myself." Several more times he says this to you. How do you respond?

❖ God desires to "remake the road that had been broken up" between human beings and God's love. Just as we cannot be brought to life unless we make our "way along that bridge" or respond to God's grace, we must help repair our own "brokenness." Imagine that your "brokenness" is the potholes and cracks between you and Jesus. Name all of the potholes and broken spots in your heart, mind, and actions: for example, "my bitterness toward my father" or "the biting comments I make to Sid."

After you have identified all of the broken places along the road to God, discuss each one with Jesus. Ask him how to repair the road.

❖ Suffering always seems to be a part of genuine love, and while we may not wish to count the cost, perhaps we do need to offer our suffering to Jesus. Recall some acts of care, service, generosity, and love that you have done in the last week or so. What small or large suffering, selflessness, or loss was required in the act of love? Offer these sufferings to God.

✧ Ponder any times when you may have refused to care for someone because it would have caused you some discomfort or suffering. Discuss these times with Jesus. Pray for more courage and hope.

✧ Pray to Jesus, the bridge to God, knowing that he always listens and responds. Make petitions, for instance: "Jesus, our bridge to God, I need to make a decision about my relationship with Sarah; help me find the way across."

God's Word

Let him kiss me with the kisses of his mouth,
for your love-making is sweeter than wine;
delicate is the fragrance of your perfume,
your name is an oil poured out, . . .

". . . Show me your face,
let me hear your voice;
for your voice is sweet
and your face is lovely." . . .
My love is mine and I am his. . . .

(Song of Songs 1:1–2; 2:14,16)

Closing prayer: Complete your meditation with these words from Catherine's *Prayers* (pp. 72–73):

O compassionate merciful Father, . . .
In mercy you grant us consolation to coax us to love,
for the creature's heart
is attracted by love.
The same mercy gives and permits sufferings and hardships
so that we might learn to know ourselves

. . . .

In mercy you preserved the scars in your Son's body
so that he might with these scars
beg for mercy for us before your majesty . . .
and for this I thank you.

✧ Meditation 7 ✧

The Crucified

Theme: Our journey, Catherine concluded, must be rooted in the teachings of Christ crucified.

Opening prayer: I thank you, God, for the love manifested in the crucifixion of Jesus.

About Catherine

Raymond of Capua writes about a vision of Jesus that Catherine described to him:

> My Apostle [Paul] has written of me [Jesus] that "for the joy set before me, I ran with eagerness to take the cross," with its load of shame and suffering. You, too, must deliberately choose the course that goes contrary to nature and brings suffering with it. It is not just a question of enduring these things with patience, but of positively embracing the cross as the very source of all your strength. The more you bear these sufferings for my sake, the more you grow in likeness to me. (Raymond, *Catherine of Siena*, p. 97)

Then Catherine was assaulted by the enemy for days. She intensified her vigils and her prayer, and suddenly she remembered how she had prayed to be able to suffer with courage. Then she spoke aloud to the spirits of evil whose presence she felt, telling them that she had made a choice to embrace suffering as the wellspring of her strength. She told them that she was willing to suffer as long as it pleased God.

At these words the demon horde turned tail and fled pell-mell, and a great light from heaven flooded the little room. And there, at the heart of the brightness, was our Lord Jesus Christ himself, nailed upon the cross and covered with his blood, in that very form in which, by his own blood, he entered into the Holy Place. From that cross he spoke to her these words: "My daughter Catherine, look at what I have suffered for your sake. Do not take it hard, then, when you too must suffer something for my sake." (*Catherine of Siena*, p. 101)

Pause: Ponder Jesus' words to Catherine.

Catherine's Words

I say we have been given a guide. I mean the only-begotten incarnate Word, God's Son, who shows us how to walk along this road that is so well lighted. He says, you know "I am way and truth and life. Whoever walks in me walks not in darkness but in light." He is Truth, and there is no falsehood in him. And what road has this gentlest of teachers built? He has built a road of hatred and of love. He so hated and despised sin that he avenged it on his own body with great pain, derision, torture, and reproach, his passion and death—and not for himself (for the poison of sin was not in him) but only as a service to us, to satisfy for our sins. He gives us back the light of grace and relieves us of the darkness that had entered our soul because of sin. (*Letters*, p. 163)

Reflection

The Crucifix of the Ecstasy was housed in Santa Christina Church in Pisa the day that the figure of Christ came to life and spoke to Catherine, searing the five wounds of the Passion onto Catherine's body. An icon of Christ is painted onto the wood frame of this cross, seeming to indicate the inseparability of the cross from the life of Jesus. The crucifix that came to life and spoke to Francis of Assisi in San Damiano—when he received the stigmata—was also an icon rather like the one at Santa Christina.

The stigmata is a sign that Catherine and Francis were so in love with Jesus, so identified with him, that they were united in his suffering. Love of God and neighbor is the key to holiness. Holiness and acceptance of suffering seem to go hand in hand because some pain accompanies love. Jesus' death was necessary to teach us about God's love for us.

✧ The Christian Scriptures tell us to put on Jesus, or to be imitators of him. Pray these words of Catherine, asking God to illumine your heart and mind as to their meaning for you: "The more you bear sufferings for my sake, the more you grow in likeness to me."

✧ Look at a crucifix, a statue, or an icon of the crucifixion. Gaze on the face of Jesus. Study the face slowly. Prayerfully touch the face. Touch the body of Jesus slowly, meditatively. What do you feel for Jesus?

✧ Bring to mind a person with whom you are in conflict or a current situation that is difficult for you. Write down or mentally inventory your feelings and any images that flash through your mind about this person or situation. Now go back and picture Jesus on the cross in the middle of this conflict or situation. Meditate on what the crucified Jesus would say to you about resolving the conflict or healing the situation.

✧ Suffering in and of itself is not a blessing. Suffering that is embraced in love is transformed. Transformed suffering can give a person strength. When we try to escape our cross, the nail holes just hurt more.

The purpose of this exercise is not to relive old hurts, but to see how you have used suffering to become more fully alive and loving. Bring to mind a time when you suffered, either physically, emotionally, or spiritually. Recollect what happened, the state you were in, who was involved, and the pain you suffered. Converse with Jesus about the suffering. Explain what you learned about him, about other people, and about yourself through the suffering. In what way was the suffering a source of conversion for you? If part of the suffering has not healed, ask Jesus to heal it.

✧ God's creation is now suffering on the cross of misuse, pollution, erosion, the extinction of species, and the stripping of the rain forests. Creation is being crucified by human greed

and neglect. How are protecting the environment and conserving natural resources ways of honoring God, the Creator? How is identifying with the suffering planet one way of being united with Jesus crucified?

✧ Light a candle. Ponder these words of Catherine: "He gives us back the light of grace and relieves us of the darkness that had entered our soul because of sin." How has Jesus' love brought you light and warmth?

God's Word

After this, Jesus knew that everything had now been completed and, so that the scripture should be completely fulfilled, he said: "I am thirsty."
   A jar full of sour wine stood there; so, putting a sponge soaked in the wine on a hyssop stick, they held it up to his mouth. After Jesus had taken the wine he said, "It is fulfilled;" and bowing his head he gave up his spirit.
   It was the Day of Preparation, and to avoid the bodies' remaining on the cross during the Sabbath . . . the Jews asked Pilate to have the legs broken and the bodies taken away. Consequently the soldiers came and broke the legs. . . . When they came to Jesus, they saw that he was already dead, and so instead of breaking his legs one of the soldiers pierced his side with a lance; and immediately there came out blood and water. This is the evidence of one who saw it . . . and he gives it so that you may believe as well. Because all this happened to fulfill the words of scripture: Not one bone of his will be broken; and again, in another place scripture says: They will look to the one whom they have pierced." (John 19:28–37)

Closing prayer: Loving God, be my companion in suffering and in joy. May I love generously, laying down my life in ways that bring your peace to the world. Amen.

✧ **Meditation 8** ✧

Continual Prayer

Theme: Catherine held firmly to the conviction that our ministry—the good that we do—flows from the depth of our prayer.

Opening prayer: In your presence, God, I pray for the continual prayer of the heart.

About Catherine

When Catherine spoke about prayer she said that the humble soul waits patiently for the flame of love. When asked how the soul waited, Catherine said, "not lazily, but in watching and constant humble prayer."

This kind of waiting taught the soul how to love without self-interest. Catherine also compared prayer to filling our cup at the fountain of love:

> Even simple folk know this. . . . If you have received my love sincerely without self-interest, you will drink your neighbor's love sincerely. It is just like a vessel that you fill at the fountain. If you take it out of the fountain to drink, the vessel is soon empty. But if you hold your vessel in the fountain while you drink, it will not get empty: Indeed it will always be full. (*The Dialogue*, pp. 120–121)

Pause: Reflect on the need to pray continually.

Catherine's Words

Catherine explains that God told her about the nature of true prayer but also that some people use prayer for self-seeking reasons, missing the real point:

> I have ordained every exercise of vocal and mental prayer to bring souls to perfect love for me and their neighbors, and to keep them in this love.
>
> So they offend me more by abandoning charity for their neighbor. For in charity for their neighbors they find me, but in their own pleasure, where they are seeking me, they will be deprived of me. Why? Because by not helping they are by that very fact diminishing their charity for their neighbors. When their charity for their neighbors is diminished, . . . so is consolation. So, those who want to gain lose, and those who are willing to lose gain. In other words, those who are willing to lose their own consolation for their neighbors' welfare receive and gain me and their neighbors, if they help and serve them lovingly. And so they enjoy the graciousness of my charity at all times. (*The Dialogue*, p. 131)

Reflection

Prayer leads us to other people because in prayer we realize God's faithful love. The soul begins to find God's greatness in Creation, in each person, and even in the tiniest things. We find the goodness that God has created in our own personhood. As we realize the goodness of all things and God's great love, God gives us the grace to nurture other people and the earth. The world becomes less frightening and more wondrous.

✧ Do you feel you are a song before God? Do you feel you are praise in God's eyes, just as you are? Pray throughout the day:
+ Let me be a song, just as I am!
+ Let me be praise in your sight.

✧ Be aware of love in your own heart. Whatever you do today, do it with love. Bake with love. Teach with love. Drive with love.

✧ We do "drink [our] neighbor's love" many times each day. Thank God for specific acts of care that have been given to you during the last several days. Make a litany of thanks, for example: "Thank you, God, for Tom's love when he cheerfully jump-started my car." "Thank you for Marcia's birthday card."

✧ Let your needs be a prayer. Desire for God, desire for nearness, and desire for intimacy spring from a sense of one's need for "more." We seek an infinite love. Pray for even more hunger for God, and pray for God to meet the needs of this hunger.

✧ What is your favorite name for God? Is it "God"? "Father"? "Mother"? "Jesus"? "Love"? "Mercy"? "Spirit"? Choose one name for God. Then close your eyes and relax.

✦ As you breathe in slowly, pray the name of God. Do the same as you slowly exhale. Pray God's name over and over.

✦ Let the name of God sink into your heart. Repeat the words as long as you like. If you find yourself becoming silent, just enjoy the reality of God's presence.

This method of prayer may be used anytime, anyplace. If this prayer becomes a habit, you may find yourself praying in your heart continually.

✧ What kind of "hungry" people do you meet? Lonely? Discouraged? Self-conscious? Reach out to a person in need. Service done in God's presence is prayer.

✧ The fruit of and inspiration for prayer is charity. As Catherine says, "those who are willing to lose gain" or "when we spend ourselves in love, we live in God's consolation." Write down any of the ways you feel you are being called to lose your life. Are you afraid of the changes this will require of you? What changes would you like to make in yourself? Converse with God about the changes you want to make in your life so that you can be more loving.

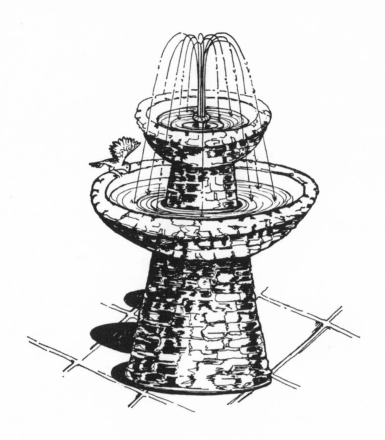

God's Word

Then Jesus said to his disciples, "If anyone wants to be a follower of mine, let him renounce himself and take up his cross and follow me. Anyone who wants to save his life will lose it; but anyone who loses his life for my sake will find it."(Matthew 16:24–25)

Closing prayer: Finish your meditation with these words from Catherine's *Prayers* (pp. 101–102):

Eternal goodness,
you want me to gaze into you
and see that you love me,
to see that you love me gratuitously,
so that I may love everyone
with the very same love.

You want me, then,
to love and serve my neighbors gratuitously,
by helping them
spiritually and materially
as much as I can. . . .

God, come to our assistance!
Amen.

✧ **Meditation 9** ✧

The Mystic Body
of the Church

Theme: In Catherine's view, the church is nothing other than Christ. Those who make up the Body of Christ accept and cooperate with God's grace to be imitators of Christ.

Opening prayer: In your holy presence, God, I pray with the church that we may become the Body of Christ on earth, setting all people on fire with love.

About Catherine

Catherine was loyal to papal authority, but she comprehended the negligence and corruption that permeated much of the church. A succession of seven French popes had lived in Avignon, France, instead of Rome. This particularly vexed Catherine because it divided the church. She was convinced that Rome was the church's true home. Determined to call the pope back to Rome, she made the long trip to the papal court in Avignon:

> Gregory, moved by Catherine's insistence, prepared for his departure to Italy. In order to make him give up this project the French King sent his brother, the Duke of Anjou, to Avignon, and the latter, who soon discovered that Catherine was the real cause of the Pope's resolution, tried

to gain her over. Catherine spent three days at his castle on the other side of the Rhône, at Villeneuve; the Duke did not convert her, but she converted him, so that he became an enthusiastic supporter. . . .

Not content with the influence that she could exercise on the Pope by direct speech, Catherine wrote a whole series of letters to him in which she refutes the objections which are continually made by the French against his journey to Rome. . . . She struggled unremittingly against the egoism in the Pope's nature, which made him irresolute and hesitating and uncertain. "Holiest and most blessed Father in Christ, sweet Jesus," she writes to him, "your unworthy and miserable [that is, someone in need of mercy] daughter Catherine strengthens you in His precious blood and desires to see you delivered from all slavish fear. . . . The fire of love burns in you. . . . Be of good courage and depart, trust in Christ Jesus; when you do that which is your duty God will be with you and none can be against you. Be a man, Father, arise! I say to you that you have nothing to fear. If you do not do your duty, then, indeed, you might have cause for fear. You ought to come to Rome, therefore come." (Jorgensen, *Saint Catherine*, pp. 232–233)

Pause: Reflect on Catherine's courage and determination.

Catherine's Words

In this passage from *The Dialogue*, God explains how Christians must serve their neighbors and thereby reform the church. In this way God can wash away the tears of the bride of Christ, the church:

> You will recall that I already told you I would fulfill your desires by giving you refreshment in your labors, that I would satisfy your anguished longings by reforming holy Church through good and holy shepherds. I will do this,

as I told you, not through war, not with the sword and violence, but through peace and calm, through my servants' tears and sweat. I have set you as workers in your own and your neighbors' souls and in the mystic body of holy Church. In yourselves you must work at virtue; in your neighbors and in the Church you must work by example and teaching. And you must offer me constant prayer for the Church and for every creature, giving birth to virtue through your neighbors. For I have already told you that every virtue and every sin is realized and intensified through your neighbors. Therefore, I want you to serve your neighbors and in this way share the fruits of your own vineyard.

Never cease offering me the incense of fragrant prayers for the salvation of souls, for I want to be merciful to the world. With your prayers and sweat and tears I will wash the face of my bride, holy Church. I showed her to you earlier as a maiden whose face was all dirtied, as if she were a leper. The clergy and the whole of Christianity are to blame for this because of their sins, though they receive their nourishment at the breast of this bride! (Pp. 159–160)

Reflection

Catherine loved the church, the bride of Christ. She was also deeply loyal to the papacy. Because of her love of the church, Catherine chided the clergy and scolded the pope. She was not blind to the defects she saw, but neither was she hopeless. When she saw illness in the church, she spoke up.

✧ Remind yourself that Jesus is present with you. Assess your own relationship with the church. Then talk with him about your feelings and concerns for the church. To aid your discussion, you might use these questions:

+ What have been your most positive experiences of church?
+ Has anything strained your relationship with the church?
+ How would you gauge your enthusiasm toward the church right now?

Open your heart and mind to Jesus about the church.

✧ In order to gain another sense of the church, ponder each of these aspects of it:

+ How does the church actively serve humankind just as Jesus did: healing, feeding, giving drink, opposing evil, and so on?

+ How is the church spreading the Word of God, teaching the Scriptures, preaching about Jesus today?

+ How is the church striving to unite people in community, just as Jesus did at the Last Supper?

✧ Catherine was an uneducated laywoman from a relatively unimportant Italian town, yet she challenged the pope to do his duty. She loved the church and, consequently, took responsibility for its health. If you were to write a letter to the pope or to some other church authority, urging reform, what would you say?

✧ Since we are the church, we are the Body of Christ on earth. Complete the following resolutions:

Today, in my everyday activities,

I can be the mouth of Christ by . . .

I can be the hands of Christ by . . .

I can be the eyes of Jesus by . . .

I can be the ears of Jesus by . . .

God's Word

And I heard what seemed to be the voices of a huge crowd, like the sound of the ocean or the great roar of thunder, answering, "Alleluia! The reign of the Lord our God Almighty has begun; let us be glad and joyful and give glory to God, because this is the time for the marriage of the Lamb. His bride is ready, and she has been able to dress herself in dazzling white linen, because her linen is made of the good deeds of the saints." The angel said, "Write this, 'Blessed are those who are invited to the wedding feast of the Lamb,'" and he added, "These words of God are true." (Revelation 19:6–9)

Closing prayer: Conclude your meditation with the following words of prayer:

Gather your people together.
Cherish your beloved.
Let us be praise in your sight.
Amen!
Amen!

✧　**Meditation 10**　✧

Mary: Loving Mother

Theme: Catherine nurtured a deep attachment to Mary, mother of Jesus, who served as a model, a mother, a friend, and a support for her.

Opening prayer: Begin your meditation with the following words of prayer:

Pray for us, O Mary.
Show us the face of your Son.
Pregnant Virgin, sign of contradiction,
Virgin Mother, containing whom the heavens cannot contain,
Heaven touched earth
and wedded in your womb.
Draw us to your breast
and take us in.

About Catherine

At the approach of harvest, before their provision of flour was exhausted, new and excellent grain was brought to the market: and hence Alessia [a young widow, follower of Catharine] intended [to] throw away the remains of the bad flour, and make bread of the new wheat just purchased, and mentioned her intention to Catharine. The latter said, "Why throw away what God has given for man's sustenance? If you do not like to eat of that bread distribute it to the poor who have none. . . . Prepare the water, and bring hither the flour that you intended throwing away, I will myself make some loaves of it, to distribute to the poor of Jesus Christ."

Catharine first kneaded the paste, and then formed from a small quantity of the bad flour, such a number of loaves and with such promptitude, that Alessia and her domestic who were looking on, could not recover from their astonishment. . . . All who partook of it not only found it free from bitterness or any unusual odor, but on the contrary declared they "had never eaten any so pleasant." . . . Catharine caused the loaves to be distributed . . . to the poor. . . .

I [Raymond] interrogated her in private concerning the details of this event, and she gave me the following answer: "I experienced an ardent wish to avoid throwing away what God had designed to bestow on us, together with an extreme compassion for the poor; I went therefore with fervor to the chest (or bin) containing the flour. My gentle Queen, the Blessed Virgin, appeared to me accompanied by Saints and Angels, she ordered me to do what I projected and deigned in her affectionate kindness to work with her royal hands in the kneading of the paste. . . ." By thus assisting Catharine, the Mother of the Word designed to show us that she gave us by her intercession the spiritual bread of salvation; just as she gave us a material and miraculous bread. (Raymond, *Saint Catharine*, 1960, pp. 217–219)

Pause: Ponder the vision of Mary kneading dough to make bread for poor people.

Catherine's Words

O Mary!
Mary!
Temple of the Trinity!
O Mary, bearer of the fire!
Mary, minister of mercy!
Mary, seedbed of the fruit!

Mary, redemptress of the human race—
for the world was redeemed
when in the Word your own flesh suffered:
Christ
by his passion redeemed us;
you,
by your grief of body and spirit.
O Mary, peaceful sea!

. . . .

Mary, fertile soil!
You, Mary, are the new-sprung plant
from whom we have the fragrant blossom,
the Word, God's only-begotten Son,
for in you, fertile soil,
was this Word sown.
You are the soil
and you are the plant.
O Mary, chariot of fire,
you bore the fire
hidden and veiled
under the ashes of your humanness. . . .

In you today
is written the eternal Father's wisdom;
in you today
our human strength and freedom are revealed.
I say that our human dignity is revealed
because if I look at you, Mary,
I see that the Holy Spirit's hand
has written the Trinity in you
by forming within you
the incarnate Word, God's only-begotten Son.
He has written for us the Father's wisdom,
which this Word is;
he has written power for us,
because he was powerful enough
to accomplish this great mystery;
and he has written for us
his own—the Holy Spirit's—mercy,

for by divine grace and mercy alone
was such a great mystery
ordained and accomplished. . . .

And even more
in you, O Mary,
our human strength and freedom
are today revealed,
for after the deliberation
of such and so great a council,
the angel was sent to you
to announce to you
the mystery of the divine counsel
and to seek to know your will,
and God's Son
did not come down into your womb
until you had given your will's consent.
He waited at the door of your will
for you to open to him;
for he wanted to come into you,
but he would never have entered
unless you had opened to him
saying,
"Here I am,
God's servant;
let it be done to me
as you have said." . . .

Today the Godhead
is joined and kneaded into one dough
with our humanity—
so securely
that this union could never be broken,
either by death
or by our thanklessness. . . .
The relationship was so entered into
and sealed
that it will never be dissolved. . . .

(*Prayers*, pp. 156, 158–159, 161, 164–165)

Reflection

God loved Mary and breathed the divine presence into her. God desires to do for all of us what God did for Mary. It is not that God is willing to accomplish great things in only one person; besides Jesus, only Mary of all creatures allowed God completely free reign in her being.

✧ What do you think God wants to accomplish in you? Are you ready to let God lead you?

✧ Select a particularly meaningful line from "Catherine's Words." Pray the line over and over. Let its message touch your heart and mind.

✧ Meditate on the image of Mary kneading dough to make bread for poor people to eat. Pounding dough can be hard work, but Mary was used to labor. How can you serve people in need through your everyday employment or through domestic activities such as making bread?

✧ Enter into the meditation on Mary, mother and nurturer, by making bread or a meal and sharing it with someone you know who is lonely, sick, or needy.

✧ Use this guided meditation to be with Mary and to meditate on what her example can teach us:
Find a comfortable, sitting position. Relax your body, breathing deeply for a good while. Close your eyes. Concentrate on breathing deeply. Let the images of the meditation flow through you.
Awesome and earthy . . . a mother and child . . . the child sucking at her breast . . . Mary . . . warm, loving, down to earth. . . . Feasting on the breast of Mary, the tiny child lies close to his mother's heart . . . drinking in his mother's milk . . . blood transformed into nourishment . . . drinking in the milk that will become his own blood . . . that will be spilled. . . . Such deep intimacy . . . between God and creatures . . . the Godhead filling the virgin womb and the milk of a human creature filling the marrow and veins of the blessed child. . . . Shepherds come . . . and worship the

child. . . . Angels sing. . . . The mother watches the people adore this child . . . and she ponders. . . .

Realizing the need to identify with humanity . . . the Godhead chose a virginal womb . . . a sacred space . . . the Godhead asks . . . asks . . . petitions . . . the woman Mary . . . "Will you please?". . . "Would you consider . . . bearing my Son?". . . The virgin consents . . . and she bears fruit. . . .

God's Word

In the sixth month the angel Gabriel was sent by God to a town in Galilee called Nazareth, to a virgin betrothed to a man named Joseph, of the House of David; and the virgin's name was Mary. He went in and said to her, "Re-

joice, you who enjoy God's favour! The Lord is with you."
She was deeply disturbed by these words and asked herself what this greeting could mean, but the angel said to her, "Mary, do not be afraid; you have won God's favour. Look! You are to conceive in your womb and bear a son, and you must name him Jesus. He will be great and will be called Son of the Most High. The Lord God will give him the throne of his ancestor David; he will rule over the House of Jacob for ever and his reign will have no end." Mary said to the angel, "But how can this come about, since I have no knowledge of man?" The angel answered, "The Holy Spirit will come upon you, and the power of the Most High will cover you with its shadow. And so the child will be holy and will be called Son of God. And I tell you this too: your cousin Elizabeth also, in her old age, has conceived a son, and she whom people called barren is now in her sixth month, for nothing is impossible to God." Mary said, "You see before you the Lord's servant, let it happen to me as you have said." And the angel left her. (Luke 1:26–38)

Closing prayer: Complete your meditation by praying these words from the "Magnificat" (*Psalms Anew*, p. 16):

My being proclaims your greatness,
and my spirit finds joy in you, God my Savior.

For you have looked upon me, your servant, in my
    lowliness;
all ages to come shall call me blessed.

God, you who are mighty, have done great things for me.
Holy is your name. . . .

✧ **Meditation 11** ✧

Union in Love

Theme: Catherine desired complete, loving union with Jesus. She imaged this mystical union as that of a bride and bridegroom. This union brings forth new love for one's neighbor.

Opening prayer: Open my heart to the mystery of love so that I may enter into the heart of God.

About Catherine

After three years of solitude, Catherine was moved by God to serve sick people and to preach the Good News, but she experienced a sense of separation from the constant intimacy she had had with Jesus. Raymond of Capua writes the following about Catherine's re-entry into public life:

> It is a bitter thing to a soul who has once tasted and seen how sweet is the Lord to be then cut off, or in any way withdrawn from the full enjoyment of that sweetness. When a spouse of the Lord is called on by him to bear children to him in the spirit, or to tend them in their needs, she must inevitably, . . . murmur to herself a protest. . . . The voice of the Bridegroom arouses the bride as she tranquilly rests in the cell of contemplation, free of the garment of temporal cares, and washed from

the stains of this world's traffic. "Open to me!" comes his urgent voice. But it is the door of the hearts of others he speaks of, not the door of her own heart; that, she has long ago flung wide for his coming. . . .

. . . At these words she would burst into tears, and in a voice broken by sobs would say: "Sweetest Lord, why are you driving me away from you? . . ."

. . . But [Jesus] replied: "Dearest daughter . . . my grace in you must now begin to bear fruit not only in yourself but in other souls as well. I have no intention whatever of parting you from myself, but rather of making sure to bind you to me all the closer, by the bond of your love for your neighbour. Remember that I have laid down two commandments of love: love of me and love of your neighbour." (Raymond, *Catherine of Siena*, pp. 113–116)

Pause: Reflect on what the Lord is asking in this passage.

Catherine's Words

Christ has made his body into a staircase, with great steps. See, his feet are nailed fast to the cross; they constitute the first step because, to begin with, the soul's desire has to be stripped of self-will, for as the feet carry the body, so desire carries the soul. Reflect that no soul will ever acquire virtue without climbing this first step. Once you have done that, you come to real, deep humility. Climb the next step without delay and you reach the open side of God's Son. Within, you will find the fathomless furnace of divine Charity. Yes, on this second step of the open side, there is a little shop, full of fragrant spices. Therein you will find the God-Man; therein, too, the soul becomes so satiated and inebriated as to become oblivious of self for, like a man intoxicated with wine, it will have eyes only for the Blood spilt with such burning love. With eager longing it presses on upwards and reaches the last step, the mouth, where it reposes in peace and quiet, savouring the peace of obedience. Like a man who falls asleep after drinking heavily and so is oblivious of both pain and pleasure, the bride of Christ, brimming over with love, sleeps in the peace of her Bridegroom. Her own feelings are so deeply asleep that she remains unruffled when assailed by tribulation and rises above undue delight in worldly prosperity; for she stripped herself of all desire of that kind back on the first step. Here [on the third step] she is conformed to Christ crucified and made one with him. (Catherine of Siena, I, Catherine, pp. 105–106)

Reflection

God invites believers into a deep, intense union of love with the Creator, the Son, and the Spirit—a call to be a daughter or son of the Creator, a spouse of Christ, and a parent in union with the Holy Spirit.

The first stage of our union with God means our conversion from selfishness to the generous love that reflects God's love of all creatures.

Becoming a spouse of Jesus is described in many ways: union with the Crucified Lover; entering the heart of Jesus; suffering; dying. Espousal love shares in the suffering of Jesus, but love overshadows the pain. However, being a spouse of Jesus demands self-surrender.

The marriage of the divine and human supports and nourishes the third phase of this union, parenting. The overshadowing of the Spirit empowered Mary to bear fruit as the mother of Jesus and the mother of the church, and this same Spirit makes love to the bride-as-church today by empowering new mothers to give forth life that radiates the presence of the holy. Women and men united with Jesus bring love into the world.

✧ Go outside for a walk. Be conscious of the earth as sacred ground.

✦ Breathe in the wind of the spirit. Ponder all the ways in which the Creator gives you life and nourishes you.

✦ Compose a litany of praise for each creation you see, hear, touch, taste, and smell, for example: "For that somber gray cloud, I thank you, Creator," or "For Lynn's cat, I thank you, Creator."

✧ Our Creator has given us other people who co-create us. Call to mind and offer to God the names of people who have shared their faith and gifts with you—who have parented you.

✧ Compose a story of how the seed of your faith was planted, nourished, tilled, and watered. You may wish to write down the story. In your story tell about the kinds of things that hindered and helped the growth of your seed.
✦ What helped rejuvenate the seed of faith? Was it compassion, a good example, an inner sense of urging?
✦ What or who served as the sun after periods of rain?
✦ What times of darkness helped your seed germinate?

✧ In the story of how your faith has grown, have you included how much your own spirit has been nourished in the act of giving to others? Have you included the gift of others listening to you or affirming you in other ways? Have you allowed others to grow by giving to you and sharing with you? Have you helped others to be "parenting figures"?

✧ Just as a wife and a husband must spend time together to nourish their marriage, people who wish to nourish their union with Jesus must spend time with him. One simple way to stay in contact is to devise ways of reminding ourselves of Jesus' constant, loving presence. Implement some practical reminders that Jesus is always with you. Maybe write his name and tape it to a mirror or put it on your desk. Formulate other simple, practical ways for you to be a better spouse of Jesus.

✧ Ponder your role as a parent. Are you able to be a mother or a father to others? How do you give forth new life? Ask yourself what you have to offer.

✧ The gifts and talents that God has given to each of us are not ours to keep. They are God's gifts, and they are meant to be shared. Catherine says God gave each of us different gifts so that instead of being self-sufficient all of us would need each other. Inventory the gifts that you are sharing with other people on a daily basis. Then talk with Jesus about how you are co-creating, co-parenting with him.

God's Word

I sleep, but my heart is awake.
I hear my love knocking.
"Open to me, my sister, my beloved,
my dove, my perfect one. . . . "

My love thrust his hand
through the hole in the door. . . .

I opened to my love,
but he had turned and gone
My soul failed at his flight,
I sought but could not find him,
I called, but he did not answer.

Where did your lover go,
O loveliest of women? . . .

My love went down to his garden,
to the beds of spices,
to pasture his flock on the grass
and gather lilies.

I belong to my love, and my love to me. . . .

Come, my love, let us go to the fields. . . .
Then I shall give you
the gift of my love.

      (Song of Songs 5:2,4,6; 6:1–3; 7:12–13)

Closing prayer: Conclude your meditation by praying these words from Catherine's *Prayers* (p. 78):

O eternal Trinity
Eternal Trinity!
O fire and deep well of charity!
O you who are madly in love
with your creature!
O eternal truth!
O eternal fire!
O eternal wisdom!

Grant us
your gentle and eternal benediction.
Amen.

✧ **Meditation 12** ✧

The Tears and the Fire of Forgiveness

Theme: The intense longing for forgiveness that Catherine experienced led to purification through the fire of longing for God and through the tears of joy.

Opening prayer: Merciful God, may I always seek wholehearted reconciliation with you through recognition of my sinfulness and your loving forgiveness.

About Catherine

After the death of her sister, [Catherine] discerned with clearer eye than ever the emptiness of the world, and began to seek again the endearments of her eternal Spouse with warmer affection and keener eagerness than before. Crying aloud her own guilt, she abased herself with Mary Magdalene, coming behind at the feet of our Lord, and shedding floods of tears. She begged him for mercy, nor would she leave off praying and grieving for her sin until, with Mary Magdalene, she would have won from him the words: "Your sins are forgiven you." From that time she began, . . . from her inmost heart, to imitate [Mary Magdalene] in seeking forgiveness for her sins. This devotion grew apace, so that in the end the Spouse of holy souls and his glorious Mother gave the Magdalene herself to Catherine as her teacher and her mother. (Raymond, *Catherine of Siena*, p. 44)

Pause: Reflect on your own desire for forgiveness.

Catherine's Words

I have told you how tears well up from the heart: The heart gathers them up from its burning desire and holds them out to the eyes. Just as green wood, when it is put into the fire, weeps tears of water in the heat because it is still green (for if it were dry it would not weep), so does the heart weep when it is made green again by the renewal of grace, after the desiccating dryness of selfishness has been drawn out of the soul. Thus are fire and tears made one in burning desire. And because desire has no end it cannot be satisfied in this life. Rather, the more it loves, the less it seems to itself to love. So love exerts a holy longing, and with that longing the eyes weep. . . .

Once the soul has left the body, tears are left behind. But loving charity has drawn to itself and consumed the tears' fruit like water in a furnace. . . . She never ceases her constant offering of her desires, blessed now and painlessly tearful. Hers are not physical tears now—for she has been dried out in the furnace—but the Holy Spirit's tears of fire. (*The Dialogue*, pp. 170–171)

Reflection

Jesus emptied himself on the cross, spilling forth blood. This final act of love demonstrated in the most perfect way Jesus' forgiveness of sins, his unconditional love, and his desire that all people be reconciled to God and to each other.

Standing before God and each other and acknowledging our destructiveness and selfishness is the first step in reconciliation. Tears empty the soul of sin and nourish the soul, bringing new life. Catherine believed that a knowledge of one's sins was a sign that God had touched a soul. Acknowledging God's love for us provides the courage to try again, to love again.

Healthy guilt leads one to empty oneself of sin, resulting in deep peace of mind and heart. Unhealthy guilt lodges inside the heart and paralyzes the individual; it distorts the truth. The truth is that we are forgiven.

✧ Reflect on your experience of God's faithful love. How do you know that God loves you? In the presence of God, acknowledge the love that has been poured out to you.

✧ Recall a time when you felt guilt. How did the guilt make you feel and act? Did you seek reconciliation? If so, how? If not, do you still wish to be forgiven? If you were reconciled, how did you feel afterwards?

✧ If you feel perplexed, sorrowful, and guilty about something now, bring to mind all the aspects of this guilt. Have you resisted reconciliation or taken steps to find forgiveness? What do you need to do? Converse with Jesus about this situation.

✧ You may wish to enter into this guided meditation that is adapted from Luke 7:36–38,44–50:

Sit comfortably. Close your eyes, and let all the tension leave your body. . . . You may need to tense your muscles and then let them relax. . . . Beginning with your feet, let the tension escape from your entire body. . . . Take your time. . . .

Now reflect on your brokenness and your sinfulness. . . . How are you destructive? . . . Picture the ways in which you are selfish. . . . What feelings surface when you contemplate your brokenness and sins? . . .

You hear that Jesus is dining with some important people in the house or apartment next door. You know that he will want to meet you, even if the others won't. . . . You walk to the door leading into the banquet that Jesus is attending. . . .

You want to meet him. . . . You want his forgiveness. . . .
Push open the door and walk over to him. . . . He sits before
you. . . . You kneel down at his feet. . . . Pour out your soul
to him. . . .

He touches you. . . . You look up into his eyes. . . .
Your gaze is held there. . . . But there is murmuring, people
complaining about you having crashed the party. . . . Jesus
raises his hand and silences them, saying to you: "You are forgiven. Your sins are forgiven.". . .

Someone from the back of the room shouts: "How can
you forgive sins? You just met this sinner.". . . Jesus replies:
"This person loves much and knows of my love. That's
enough.". . . Turning back to you, he says gently, "Go, friend,
go into peace.". . .

You kiss his hand away, . . . and standing, you walk
from the room. . . . As you walk away, a storm of emotions
washes over you.

✧ Spend some time listening to Jesus say to you over
and over, "Your sins are forgiven because you have loved
much."

God's Word

One of the Pharisees invited [Jesus] to a meal. When he
arrived at the Pharisee's house and took his place at table,
suddenly a woman came in, who had a bad name in the
town. She had heard he was dining with the Pharisee and
had brought with her an alabaster jar of ointment. She
waited behind him at his feet, weeping, and her tears fell
on his feet, and she wiped them away with her hair; then
she covered his feet with kisses and anointed them with
the ointment. . . . Then he turned to the woman and
said to Simon [the Pharisee], "You see this woman? I
came into your house, and you poured no water over my
feet, but she has poured out her tears over my feet and
wiped them away with her hair. You gave me no kiss, but
she has been covering my feet with kisses ever since I
came in. You did not anoint my head with oil, but she has
anointed my feet with ointment. For this reason I tell you

that her sins, many as they are, have been forgiven her, because she has shown such great love. It is someone who is forgiven little who shows little love." Then he said to her, "Your sins are forgiven." Those who were with him at table began to say to themselves, "Who is this man, that even forgives sins?" But he said to the woman, "Your faith has saved you; go in peace." (Luke 7:36–50)

Closing prayer: Conclude your meditation with these words of prayer:

Jesus . . . weeping over Jerusalem,
Jesus . . . waiting at the tomb of Lazarus,
Jesus . . . in the garden, sweating blood,
Jesus . . . crying out to heaven from the cross.
Jesus . . . revealing the heart of God.
Show us your face,
stained with sweat,
blazing with fire.
Silent tears, speak to me of your love and forgiveness.

✧ Meditation 13 ✧

Bread of Life
and Cup of Blessing

Theme: The experience of communion was, for Catherine, a time of union with God. The Bread of Life sustained Catherine in her work with sick people, in her visits to prisoners, and in all of her ministry.

Opening prayer: May I approach the mystery of your love, my God, enter into your embrace, and be nourished by the Body and Blood of Jesus.

About Catherine

When Catherine visited sick people and prisoners, counseled the doubtful, and attended to the family members of plague victims, she was buoyed along by the strength and courage she received from communion with God at Eucharist.

Raymond described Catherine's reliance on communion this way:

> Inspired by our Lord himself, she took on the practice of frequent Communion. For the rest of her life it remained her custom to approach the sacred altar as frequently as possible, and there to receive from the hand of the priest, in the Blessed Sacrament, Christ our Lord—that living God in whom her heart and her flesh exulted for joy. . . .

By the force of faith with which she took this holy Food, she found it far more capable . . . of giving her strength to bear that burning charity which kept growing ever more fervent in the furnace of her heart, as the breath of the Holy Spirit kept blowing it day by day into a consuming flame. In this way the habit of receiving Communion practically every day struck root in her and became part of her life. Naturally, it often happened, through sickness or through occupations arising out of her work for souls, that she was prevented from receiving daily. But her longing for more and more frequent Communion was so intense that when she could not receive it her very body felt the deprivation, and her forces seemed to droop. For as her body shared the overflow of the energies of her spirit, so it could not but be weakened when her spiritual vitality flagged for the lack of the Bread of Life. (Raymond, *Catherine of Siena*, p. 160)

Pause: Reflect on the place of communion in your life.

Catherine's Words

I beg you, for the love of Christ crucified, to respond with joy and eager longing to the invitation to this glorious wedding-feast [the Eucharist], with its promise of sweetness, joy and every delight. At this feast we leave all uncleanness behind; released from sin and suffering, we dine at the table of the Lamb, where the Lamb himself is both our food and our servant. The Father, you see, is our table, bearing everything that is—except sin, which is not in him. The Word, God's Son, has made himself our food, roasted in the blazing fire of charity, while the servant at the table is that very charity, the Holy Spirit, who gave and gives us God with [the Godhead's] own hands. (Catherine of Siena, *I, Catherine*, p. 91)

Reflection

Bread and wine are literally nourishing food, basic to the diet of humans for millenia. To the believer, bread and wine become the Bread and Wine of Life, the Body and Blood of Jesus that nourishes our whole personhood. When we eat food, it becomes the tissue of which we are composed; it becomes us. When we eat the food of eternal life, it becomes infused throughout our whole being. Catherine believed so firmly in this that she, reportedly, weakened physically when she could not partake of communion.

The Eucharist is often compared to a wedding feast. The word *Eucharist* is derived from the Greek words for "giving thanks." Indeed, if we believe that we are united with Jesus in the Eucharist, we are united with Jesus even more intimately than a man and woman who are wed. Giving thanks and celebration are fitting responses to our union with Jesus.

✧ Think of one word that best summarizes the meaning of the Eucharist for you right now. Ponder, perhaps by writing in your journal if you keep one, why this word encapsulates your belief.

✧ Bring a piece of bread and maybe a little glass of wine to your place of prayer. Very slowly eat the bread and drink the wine. Relax and imagine how the bread and wine are absorbed into your whole body to become part of you. Then spend time meditating on these questions:

✦ When I receive communion, do I sense the same absorption of the Bread and Wine of Life into my life? Do I believe that just as bread and wine can be transformed into energy, so too is the Bread and Wine of Life transformed into energy for goodness and justice?

✧ Concentrate on these prayer words—"Bread of Life and Cup of Blessing." Repeat the words over and over again, welcoming Jesus into your body, soul, and mind.

✧ The Eucharist is a communal meal, which brings people together and is the means of celebrating community. Are there ways in which your own participation in the Eucharist can be more celebrative and a source of unity in your community?

✧ Converse with Jesus about these words of Raymond: the Eucharist gave her "strength to bear that burning charity which kept growing ever more fervent in the furnace of her heart." Ask Jesus how you can grow in strength to burn with charity.

God's Word

. . . Jesus took bread, and when he had said the blessing he broke it and gave it to the disciples. "Take it and eat," he said, "this is my body." Then he took a cup, and when he had given thanks he handed it to them saying, "Drink from this, all of you, for this is my blood, the blood of the covenant, poured out for many for the forgiveness of sins." (Matthew 26:26–28)

Closing prayer: Complete your meditation using these words of prayer:

Body broken
and
Blood poured
out.

Jesus.
Jesus.
Jesus.

✧ Meditation 14 ✧

Proclaiming Peace

Theme: Warring factions sought Catherine's assistance in making peace. Hearing Jesus' call in these requests, Catherine strove to arbitrate disputes and reunite antagonists, despite the dangers to herself.

Opening prayer: I pray for the gift of inner peace, a peace that bears fruits of goodwill, reconciliation, and forgiveness, a peace that brings harmony to the community of humankind.

About Catherine

A long, bitter, and complicated dispute raged between the papacy and the city-state of Florence. At one point the pope tried to force Florence to its knees by placing it under interdict. The Florentines used Catherine as an intermediary, sending her to Avignon to negotiate with the pope. Despite her efforts, the Florentines repudiated her work later on. When fighting recommenced in 1378, the pope called on Catherine:

> Raymond tells how, one Sunday morning in Rome, after he had been preaching, he was sent for by the Pope and had to report himself immediately after his midday meal. "It has been written to me," Gregory told the Dominican, "that if Catherine of Siena went to Florence, peace would

be made." "Not only Catherine, but all of us are ready to suffer even martyrdom, if your Holiness commands it," was Raymond's evasive answer. "I do not want you to go to Florence," the Pope answered, "they will treat you ill. But I do not think they will harm Catherine, in part because she is a woman, and in part because they revere her." The audience concluded in the Dominican being told to report himself all ready the next morning with the . . . required papers for Catherine's mission. (Jorgensen, *Saint Catherine*, pp. 280–281)

Pause: Spend some moments considering how you have been a peacemaker.

Catherine's Words

Catherine responded to Pope Gregory's invitation, but interestingly, Catherine begins by chiding and instructing the pontiff, who shared the blame for the war with Florence:

> In the name of Jesus Christ Crucified and of Sweet Mary Most Holy, holy and reverend father in Christ sweet Jesus, your unworthy daughter Catherine, servant and slave of the servants of Jesus Christ, writes your Holiness in His precious blood with desire to see you achieve peace, having peace yourself and your children around you. That is the peace God requires of you, and he wants you to do what you can, . . . strike them more with your staff of kindness, love and peace rather than the rod of war; and you will truly regain them spiritually and temporally. Wedging my soul between you and God, with great hunger for our salvation and the reform of holy Church and the good of the entire world, it seems that God reveals no other remedy than that of peace. Peace, peace then, for the love of Christ Crucified! And do not consider the ignorance, blindness and pride of your children. With peace you will cast out war and malice of heart and division, and unite them to yourself. Thus by virtue you will throw out the devil. (Letter 209, trans. Sister Mary Jeremiah Gillett)

Reflection

Catherine assisted in the peace process between Florence and the pope, but she also taught that inner strife is a source of discord in the world and in the church. Inner peace can be a source of harmony among people and nations.

Humans tend to project the causes of turmoil onto other people. Catherine calls the pope, the citizens of Florence, Siena, and Rome, and even her confessors to walk through their hearts and to see where the fault for many divisive situations lies within them.

Catherine's gift as a peacemaker was largely rooted in her ability to identify the true sources of discord. On the other hand, she had the compassion and understanding that came from wrestling with her own lack of peace.

✧ Are there any individuals who stir up your anger and bitterness? List each person on paper or in your mind and recall the feelings that come to you when you think of each one. Name your reactions or behaviors that result from these feelings. Then recall God's presence with you and talk with God about how to bring peace to these relationships.

✧ Imagine that Catherine was writing her letter to you and not to the pope. Ponder what she says in the letter that applies to you. Write a response to her; imagine that she will read your letter.

✧ In your place of work, congregation, family, or neighborhood, are there ways in which you could be a peacemaker?

✧ Without justice, peace is impossible. Do injustices exist in your place of work or in your local community? Are you being called to strive for justice? Spend some time with Jesus talking about what you can do.

✧ Regularly pray this prayer or one of your own: "Lamb of God, fill me with peace, show me the way to peacemaking."

God's Word

In the evening of that same day, the first day of the week, the doors were closed in the room where the disciples were, for fear of the Jews. Jesus came and stood among them. He said to them, "Peace be with you," and, after saying this, he showed them his hands and his side. The disciples were filled with joy at seeing the Lord, and he said to them again, "Peace be with you."

"As the Father sent me,
so am I sending you."

After saying this he breathed on them and said:

Receive the Holy Spirit.
If you forgive anyone's sins,
they are forgiven. . . .

(John 20:19–23)

Closing prayer: God looked on Catherine and proclaimed this blessing:

I, the sea of peace, . . .
share with you, with each of you
according to your own capacity.
I fill you
and do not leave you empty.

(*The Dialogue*, p. 360)

The Key of Obedience

Theme: Central to Catherine's spirituality is obedience to the word of God. By following Jesus' example, we have life. She calls obedience "the key" that permits us to pass through the world's darkness and to unlock heaven.

Opening prayer: I ask for the spirit of obedience and for the courage to lay down my life in love for God and others.

About Catherine

Raymond of Capua asked Catherine how she remained so cheerful despite the heavy workload her family had given her and the contempt they had shown toward her. She replied that in her imagination,

> she vividly pictured her father as representing our Lord and Saviour Jesus Christ; her mother as his most glorious Mother Mary; her brothers and the rest of the household as his apostles and disciples. Picturing them in this fashion she was able to render them a cheerful and unfailing service which filled them with astonishment. Another advantage that followed was that, as she went about her tasks, she kept her mind fixed on her Spouse, regarding herself as in reality serving him. Outwardly she was in the kitchen; inwardly in the Holy of Holies. Outwardly

she was waiting at table; inwardly her soul was feasting on the presence of her Saviour. (Raymond, *Catherine of Siena*, pp. 47–48)

Pause: Reflect briefly on Catherine's example of obedience.

Catherine's Words

Catherine told her companions that she wondered about the role of obedience in her own life but that God had said to her:

> You ask me where you may find obedience. . . . My answer is that you will find it in its fullness in the gentle loving Word, my only-begotten Son. His obedience was so ready that to realize it he ran to his shameful death on the cross.
>
> What takes obedience away?
>
> Look at the first man. What took away the obedience that I the eternal Father had laid on him was the pride that came from his selfish love. . . . [This] eternal life, which had been locked by Adam's disobedience, was unlocked by the key of obedience.
>
> [How did this happen?]
>
> When I saw that humankind, whom I so loved, were not returning to me their end, my infinite goodness constrained me to put the key of obedience into the hand of the gentle loving Word, my Truth, and he like a doorman unlocked heaven's gate. . . .
>
> Each of you individually has it, the very Word's key. . . . You must, then, carry the key in your hand. . . . The blood of the Lamb by whose power the key of obedience shed its rust. . . . Obedience . . . has opened [heaven] for you by the power of the blood. (*The Dialogue*, pp. 327–328, 330, 333)

Reflection

The word *obedience* comes from a Latin word meaning "to listen." For Catherine and all Christians, obedience means listening to God's call and following God's will. When Jesus asked if the cup of suffering could be taken away, he listened to God and surrendered his own will by entering into the will of God.

The will of God manifests itself in the Bible, in the signs of the times, in the needs of the human family, and through the church. We discern God's will by listening to all of these sources and then praying that God will lead us to correct decisions and responses. Obedience is an active, searching process.

✧ Spend some time praying this phrase in harmony with your slow, rhythmic breathing: "Not my will, but yours, O God."

✧ Catherine knew that doing God's will oftentimes precedes understanding; we must be obedient before we see God's plan for us. Recall things that you did not understand until you experienced them: sickness, being in love, grief, giving birth, emotional pain, peace. What other experiences have you gone through that have led to new understanding or appreciation? What was God telling you through each of these experiences?

✧ Sometimes we are tempted to pre-empt God's will by turning a blind eye to ideas, people, or events.

List some experiences, people, or ideas to which you have been drawn but from which you have turned away, even though you believed that the experience could have led to an increased understanding of God's world or of yourself. After you have completed your list, try to explain to God and yourself why you turned away. Why were you, perhaps, afraid? What did you feel you might lose? Dialog with the Holy Spirit about how you could be more open to God's will.

✧ Visiting the sick, feeding the hungry, listening to the lonely, paying a just wage, and giving someone a second chance are all part of God's will for us as described in the Scriptures. Jesus summarized his will for us in the two great commandments to love God and love our neighbors as ourselves. How are you surrendering to God's will as seen in the Scriptures? Examine your behavior for the last several days. Do you seek God's will by reading the Scriptures regularly?

✧ Before we can surrender to God's will, we must have faith in God's complete love for us. We need to believe that the will of God as seen in the Word and in the requests for help from other people is good for others and for ourselves. We need to remind ourselves of God's love for us; pray the words "God is love" many times throughout the day. The God who loves us will never ask for anything but love from us.

God's Word

So if in Christ there is anything that will move you, any incentive in love, any fellowship in the Spirit, any warmth or sympathy—I appeal to you, make my joy complete by being of a single mind. . . . Nothing is to be done out of jealousy or vanity; instead, out of humility of mind everyone should give preference to others, everyone pursuing not selfish interests but those of others. Make your own the mind of Christ Jesus:

Who, being in the form of God,
did not count equality with God
something to be grasped.

But he emptied himself,
taking the form of a slave,
becoming as human beings are;
and being in every way like a human being,
he was humbler yet,
even to accepting death, death on a cross.

And for this God raised him high,
and gave him the name
which is above all other names;

so that all beings
in the heavens, on earth and in the underworld,
should bend the knee at the name of Jesus

and that every tongue should acknowledge
Jesus Christ as Lord,
to the glory of God the Father.

(Philippians 2:1–11)

Closing prayer: Complete your meditation with these words from Catherine's *Prayers* (p. 176):

O gentle eternal God,
[You] gave us the Word
with the bait of his humanity,
and you caught both us and the devil,
by the power not of humanity
but of divinity.
By thus making yourself small
you have made us great.

. . . .

By stripping yourself of life
you have clothed us in grace.

. . . .

By being stretched out on the cross
you have embraced us.
For us
you have made a cavern in your open side,
where we might have a refuge

. . . .

There we have found the bath
in which we have washed our soul's face clean
of the leprosy of sin.
O delightful love!
O fire!
O deep well of charity!

I thank you,
I thank you.

LO·V·E

✧ For Further Reading ✧

Baldwin, Anne B. *Catherine of Siena: A Biography*. Huntington, IN: Our Sunday Visitor, 1987.

Catherine of Siena. *Catherine of Siena: The Dialogue*. Trans. Suzanne Noffke. New York: Paulist Press, 1980.

————. *The Letters of St. Catherine of Siena*. Trans. Suzanne Noffke. Binghamton, NY: Medieval and Renaissance Texts and Studies, 1988.

————. *The Prayers of Catherine of Siena*. Ed. Suzanne Noffke. New York: Paulist Press, 1983.

————. *I, Catherine: Selected Writings of St. Catherine of Siena*. Ed. Kenelm Foster and Mary John Ronayne. London: Collins, 1980.

Fatula, Mary Ann. *Catherine of Siena's Way*. Vol. 4 of *The Way of the Christian Mystics*. Wilmington, DE: Michael Glazier, 1987.

Follmar, Mary Ann. *The Steps of Love in the Dialogue of St. Catherine of Siena*. Petersham, MA: Saint Bede's Publications, 1987.

Jorgensen, Johannes. *Saint Catherine of Siena*. Trans. Ingeborg Lund. London, New York, and Toronto: Longmans, Green, and Co., 1938.

Raymond of Capua. *The Life of Catherine of Siena*. Trans. Conleth Kearns. Wilmington, DE: Michael Glazier, 1980.

Acknowledgments (*continued*)

The psalms quoted on pages 55 and 81 are from *Psalms Anew: In Inclusive Language*, compiled by Nancy Schreck and Maureen Leach. (Winona, MN: Saint Mary's Press, 1986). Used by permission of the publisher. All rights reserved.

All other scriptural excerpts in this book are from the New Jerusalem Bible. Copyright © 1985 by Darton, Longman & Todd, Ltd., London, and Doubleday, a division of Bantam, Doubleday, Dell Publishing Group, Inc., New York. Reprinted by permission.

Excerpts on pages 83–84 and 94 are from *I, Catherine: Selected Writings of St. Catherine of Siena*, edited and translated by Kenelm Foster, OP, and Mary John Ronayne, OP (Saint James's Place, London: William Collins Sons & Company, Ltd., 1980), pages 105–106 and 91, respectively. Copyright © 1980 by Kenelm Foster. Used with permission from the publisher.

Excerpts on pages 32, 37–38, 42, 52, 57–58, 65, 66, 71–72, 89, 101, and 103 are from *Catherine of Siena: The Dialogue*, translation and introduction by Suzanne Noffke, OP, preface by Giuliana Cavallini (New York: Paulist Press, 1980), pages 152–153; 277; 121; 185; 59; 120–121; 131; 159–160; 170–171; 360; 327–328, 330, 333; respectively. Copyright © 1980 by t.he Missionary Society of Saint Paul the Apostle in the State of New York. Used with permission from the publisher.

Excerpts on pages 35, 40, 50, 55, 59, 68–69, 76–78, 87, and 106 are from *The Prayers of Catherine of Siena*, edited by Suzanne Noffke, OP (New York: Paulist Press, 1983), pages 105; 187–188; 186–188; 114; 72–73; 101–102; 156, 158–159, 161, 164–165; 78; and 176; respectively. Copyright © 1983 by Suzanne Noffke, OP. Used with permission from the publisher.

The letters of Catherine of Siena on pages 37 and 98 were translated by Sister Mary Jeremiah Gillett, OP, Monastery of the Infant Jesus, Lufkin, TX. Used with permission.

Excerpts on pages 46, 51–52, 60, 61, 82–83, 88–89, 93–94, and 102–103 are from *The Life of Catherine of Siena*, by Raymond of Capua, translated, introduced, and annotated by Conleth Kearns, OP, preface by Vincent de Couesnongle, OP (Wilmington, DE: Michael Glazier, Inc., 1980), pages 46–47, 81–82, 97, 101, 113–116, 44, 160, and 47–48, respectively. Copyright © 1980 by Conleth Kearns. Reprinted with permission from the

Titles in the Companions for the Journey Series

Praying with Catherine of Siena
Praying with Clare of Assisi
Praying with Dominic
Praying with Dorothy Day
Praying with Elizabeth Seton
Praying with Francis of Assisi
Praying with Hildegard of Bingen
Praying with Ignatius of Loyola
Praying with John Baptist de La Salle
Praying with John of the Cross
Praying with Julian of Norwich
Praying with Louise de Marillac   Forthcoming
Praying with Teilhard de Chardin   Forthcoming
Praying with Teresa of Ávila
Praying with Thérèse of Lisieux
Praying with Thomas Merton
Praying with Vincent de Paul

Order from your local religious bookstore or from

Saint Mary's Press
702 TERRACE HEIGHTS
WINONA MN 55987-1320
USA
1-800-533-8095